PARENTS,
TEENS AND SEX

THE
BIG
TALK
BOOK

10 STEPS TO EMPOWER YOUR TEEN TO
CHOOSE THE BEST - ABSTINENCE UNTIL MARRIAGE

SECOND EDITION

BRUCE COOK

Acknowledgments

Editing and Research – Ann B. Cannon

Text and Cover Design – Bart Shelnutt, Shelnutt Design

Illustrations – Robbie Short

Content Review – Donna Cook, Marcia Papst, Melanie Smallie

Choosing the Best Publishing gratefully acknowledges Teen Advisors, Inc. and Friends First for identifying and providing access to the teens who participated in our national survey. The publisher also wishes to thank the Medical Institute of Sexual Health for the STD slides used in Appendix B.

Published by
Choosing the Best, LLC
2625 Cumberland Parkway, N.E.
Suite 200
Marietta, Georgia 30339-3911

Library of Congress Cataloguing-in-Publication Data
Cook, Bruce
Parents, Teens and SEX: The BIG TALK Book *10 Steps to Empower Your Teen to Choose the Best – Abstinence Until Marriage* / by Bruce Cook
    p. cm
    ISBN 0-9724890-6-1
1. Parents and teenagers-United States.   2. Parenting-United States.
3. Family-United States.   4. Teenagers-United States.
5. Sexual Abstinence-United States.   I. Title.   II. Series.

Printed in the United States of America

ISBN 0-9724890-6-1

Dedication

To my son, Brannon, and my daughter, Natalie,
who provided the motivation
and
my wife, Donna, who provided the inspiration

About *Choosing the Best*

Founded in 1993, *Choosing the Best* is a national leader in abstinence-focused sex and relationship education. Our research-based, medical learning model motivates students through relationship education, refusal-skill coaching, character education, and parent-teen interviews. We offer four programs specifically tailored for middle and high school teens:

Choosing the Best **WAY — 6th Grade.** Created for lower middle school students, this six-lesson curriculum gives students age-appropriate insight into what's happening to their changing bodies and emotions, explores their new interest in the opposite sex, and teaches abstinence as the best WAY.

Choosing the Best **PATH — 7th and 8th Grades.** This dynamic eight-lesson curriculum captivates upper middle school students. After students are challenged to make a commitment to sexual abstinence, additional lessons help them learn how to stay committed to the best PATH.

Choosing the Best **LIFE — 8th and 9th Grades.** This high-impact eight-lesson curriculum for upper middle school and lower high school students engages the heart as well as the head and teaches students that abstinence is the best choice for LIFE.

Choosing the Best **SOUL MATE — 11th and 12th Grades.** Created for upper high school students, this five-lesson curriculum provides older students with the interpersonal skills essential for successful relationships of all kinds and ultimately, for a successful marriage. A logical sequel to *Choosing the Best* abstinence programs for younger teens, SOUL MATE continues to emphasize that sexual abstinence is a critical step to prepare for a lifelong relationship.

Parents are the single most important factor in a teen's sexual decision-making. That's why *Choosing the Best* offers a parent education program as well as a parent book that help empower parents to encourage their teens to choose abstinence:

PARENT PREP — This powerful parent education program provides maximum impact and is ideal for PTA presentations, parents groups, and teacher in-service training.

Parents, Teens and SEX: The BIG TALK Book — An important resource for every parent of teenagers, this book offers ten critical steps parents can take to help empower their teens to choose abstinence until marriage.

For more information on these products and *Choosing the Best* training workshops and materials, contact *Choosing the Best* at 1-800-774-BEST, or visit www.choosingthebest.org.

Contents

INTRODUCTION

You Are More Important Than You Think!

The Challenging Teen Years

Almost overnight, our son, Brannon, changed from an easy-going, obedient middle schooler to a full-blown TEENAGER with a mind of his own! Normal conversation turned into grunts. Hugs resulted in resistance. Bedroom doors suddenly slammed shut. Friends dominated all phases of his life. And, Brannon greeted questions like: "Where are you going?" "When will you be home?" "Who are you going with?" with the pervasive response: "I don't know."

Our son's greatest fear was that his friends would see him while he hung out with his parents. On more than one occasion, Brannon would slide below eye level in the car when his friends came into view. For Brannon, all of these fears and feelings were normal and natural as he was becoming an adult person, separate from us. But for us as parents, going through this for the first time with our oldest child, there was a great sense of helplessness. Parenting approaches that once worked were no longer effective. We felt that our days of influencing and guiding our new, young "adult" were over.

Around the same time, we became acutely aware of the temptations in the world. These could be potential stumbling blocks for our "little" boy – who was no longer little, but showed signs of budding manhood. Stories circulated among parents about young teens drinking, having sex, and participating in other at-risk behaviors.

It's at this point that braver parents may try to have a BIG TALK about sex – not the "birds and the bees" basic discussion about sex, but the one that covers teen sexuality beyond the birds and the bees. And what is the typical response to this attempt? Eyes roll so quickly, you'd think they were on a merry-go-round, and the "Ah, mom!" "Ah, dad!" flowing rapidly. And then, of course, the "I already know all this" and "Are we finished yet?" No wonder parents throw up their hands, feeling there is nothing they can do.

You Are Important!

Teens may grimace, shuffle, and look bored, but research shows that they look to parents for guidance and direction, especially in the area of sexuality. In fact, countless studies confirm that teens view parents as the **single most significant influence** in developing character and values and in sexual decision making.

- Among 15- to 17-year-olds who are not sexually active, 64 percent said that the major reason they decided to wait was because of what their parents might think.[1]
- Up to 80 percent of these same teens said that parents influenced their decision making about sex and relationships.[2]
- Another study found that parents were three times more influential than friends in a teen's life.[3]
- In fact, 46 percent of the teens see a family member as a role model.[4]
- When asked to rank 14 sources of influence that helped teens decide between right and wrong, teens listed parents as being the most influential.[5]
- 45 percent of teenagers say that their parents had the biggest influence on their sexual behavior, whereas 31 percent say their friends are the biggest influence.[6]
- 88 percent of teenagers said that it would be much easier for them to postpone sexual activity if they were able to have more open, honest conversations about these topics with their parents. 40 percent of teenagers said they had not had an open, honest conversation with their parents about sex.[7]

Research studies done for *Choosing the Best* and conducted by Northwestern University School of Medicine and a leading researcher at Georgia Institute of Technology found four variables that identified students who were more than twice as likely to be sexually active than their peers. The first two variables involved parents:

- Not having two parents in the home
- Perceived parental approval of teen sex
- Smoking
- Drinking and getting drunk[8]

Using Teen Experts for Tips

To find out what factors influenced teens to be sexually abstinent, *Choosing the Best* surveyed 100 teens from all over the country who have chosen to be abstinent until marriage. The survey was used to find out what influenced each teen to be abstinent and what advice the teens would give to parents to encourage their teenagers to be abstinent. Their candid responses have shaped the 10 steps found in this book. In the survey, the highest rated factor influencing their decision to be abstinent until marriage was **parental expectations**. Here's what these teens relate about parental expectations:

"They wanted me to wait because they wanted me to have a healthy relationship. We had open discussions about where the lines are drawn."

"They wanted the best for me and wanted me to experience the least amount of pain."

"They don't want me getting pregnant or [contracting] an STD – be abstinent."

"My parents are both high school dropouts due to sex. They don't want me to repeat the mistake."

"They said [to] be abstinent. They said they were proud of me, keep up the good work, do the right things, and do my best."

"They explained to me the plan was for me to remain pure for my husband and to be patient for my husband to come. They explained the mistakes they made and how they want something better for me."

The parents of these teens have two things in common: they believe that abstinence until marriage is best for their child, and they communicate that message often.

Meanwhile, Back on the Ranch . . .

Sex education! I couldn't believe the assignment my wife Donna and Brannon's school. When I was in school, health and safety involved making sure the school patrols had their white badges on so they could stop traffic and help students safely cross the streets. Now, the school wanted parents to select sex education material to be taught in the ninth-grade, starting with our son's class, which would be the first to use this new curriculum. The year was 1992. AIDS and sexually transmitted diseases made headlines as growing epidemics. In addition, teen pregnancies continued to increase among young teens.

The school's committee, made up of parents, teachers, and administrators, unanimously agreed to encourage abstinence among our students. A search of existing curricula resulted in finding programs that were either too "preachy" or those that encouraged "safe sex" through the use of condoms.

I decided that we would write our own sex-education curriculum. With the help of two school counselors, several medical experts and other resources – including our friend Bill Roper, who headed the Centers for Disease Control and Prevention in Atlanta at the time – and using my son's class as guinea pigs, the first *Choosing the Best* curriculum was developed.

Choosing the Best has grown from a single program in middle school to a four year comprehensive curriculum, featuring **Choosing the Best** WAY for lower middle school, **Choosing the Best** PATH for upper middle school, **Choosing the Best** LIFE for upper middle school or lower high school, and **Choosing the Best** SOUL MATE for upper high school. An independent study of *Choosing the Best* indicated, after 12 months, a 47 percent reduction in the initiation of teen sex among those students who received the *Choosing the Best* program compared to a control group who did not receive the program. Today more than 1 million students nationwide have completed *Choosing the Best*.

Parents Must Lead!

After a decade in the abstinence-education arena, I am convinced that, although we can and should provide effective abstinence education in our schools, parents must take the lead. Parents must accept responsibility for guiding their teens to choose abstinence until marriage. That's why I've written this book – to equip you as a parent to talk with your teen, beyond the "birds and the bees." How tempting it is to sit back and let schools or religious institutions teach our teens.

But you are more important than you think. This seems difficult to believe when your teen rolls his eyes at your attempts to communicate, or when your teen apathetically responds with "I don't know" when asked what he or she thinks. But, you can make a difference!

How to Have the BIG TALK – In 10 Engaging Discussions

Want to know how to gain the maximum benefit from this book? At the end of each step is a section called "**Parent: Let's Think About It!**" The questions and activities in this section give you a chance to reflect on the ideas presented in that step. Following that section is "**Parent and Teen: Let's Talk About It**," a hands-on way to discuss each topic with your teen. Each discussion segment will take approximately 30 minutes and builds on the previous step. You may want to set up a weekly time to work through each step with your teen. Here's another idea for going through the discussion sections – take your teen on a weekend retreat. Go fishing or hiking or skiing. Sprinkle in fun activities with the discussions.

I promise you that the opportunity to interact with your teen about the key issues of teen sexuality will be a significant investment in your teen's life and future. Abstinence until marriage provides the greatest degree of freedom for your son or daughter – freedom to pursue life goals and dreams, and freedom from the fear of teen pregnancy, sexually transmitted diseases, and the negative emotional effects associated with at-risk sexual behavior.

I know this will be a great adventure in talking to your teen about sexual abstinence. Have a great relationship adventure with your teen! Now, on to Step One.

PARENTS, TEENS AND SEX

THE BIG TALK BOOK

Step One

Be Informed

Things Really Have Changed!

The gentleman sitting across the table from me was a well-known lawyer in a large metropolitan city. His knowledge and savvy had helped him win numerous high profile cases. In addition, he and I had gone through the teen parenting years together. We often had shared the same challenges of sleepless nights and basic concerns associated with rearing teens. But he was blown away when I shared the reality of teens and sex today. Like many parents, he was unaware of the highly charged sexual world that today's teenagers face.

This world is vastly different, and much more complex than the one in which many of us grew up. Sex is no longer whispered about behind closed doors; it is openly discussed each night on TV. That goodnight kiss on the first date has been replaced by more overt sexual activity, which is not only accepted, but expected. Even institutions like schools have lost their moral footings.

The Really Bad News

The most common sexual activity of 13-year-olds is kissing. But, by the time of high school graduation, or 18 years of age:

> • More than 60 percent of teens will have had sexual intercourse.[1]

> • Twenty-five percent of sexually active teens will have contracted a sexually transmitted disease[2] – and most won't even know it!

• Twenty percent of sexually active girls will have been pregnant.[3]

One common message bombards teens everyday, from every side – "Sexual activity for teens is a part of growing up. It's normal, natural and has no consequences. So, do what feels right!" Only later do teens discover the truth that sex outside of marriage can bring heartache and other strong emotional consequences. It might even result in the devastation of a teen pregnancy or a lifelong sexually transmitted disease.

Five Major Influences

To help your teen deal with this sexual world, you need to explore the influences that cause these at-risk behaviors. Some influences seem obvious. Others may offer new thoughts. Remember: healthy, normal teens struggle with these five major pressures to become sexually active every day.

Influence #1: Hormones

Puberty happens to everyone. It is the time when the body matures from a child into the body of an adult that is capable of reproduction. For a boy, puberty starts with the enlargement of the testicles and the production of sperm. This may occur between the ages of 10 and 16. For a girl, puberty is marked by breast development and the start of menstruation. This may start as young as 8, but more often it occurs around 11 or 12 years of age. In fact, one writer observed that young girls today can produce babies at an age much younger than their grandmothers had their first periods.[4]

Emotional highs and lows accompany the numerous physical changes. As the sex hormones of testosterone in the male and estrogen in the female are released, intense sexual feelings occur. All those raging

Let's look at what several of the 100 teen experts we interviewed for this book said about the greatest pressures put on them to be sexually active:

"Society is telling me to just do it"

"The physical attraction to a guy – my hormones"

"Pressure from my friends"

"Porn on the Internet and on videos"

"Socially accepted fact that sex is a part of a love relationship"

"The greatest pressures are the girls – their behaviors, styles of living and my hormones"

"Pressure from my boyfriend to have sex to prove my love to him"

"Hot guys!!! They say they love you."

hormones lead to a natural curiosity about the opposite sex. Girls who once raced around at recess chasing boys suddenly exude tremendous powers of attraction and have boys chasing them. Guys who once preferred skateboards to girls now find they can attract girls with little effort.

Sexual feelings are normal, natural and part of growing up. For example, the average teenage boy has five to six hormonal surges each day. With puberty beginning earlier (8 to 12 years for girls and 10 to 16 years for boys[5]), and marriage occurring later (women marry around the age of 25, guys around the age of 27[6]), young people face a longer period of time to hold back those raging hormones. Hormones, however, do not have to control a teen. Unlike animals, which mate because of biological instincts, teens can learn to delay natural urges in order to gain long-term benefits and healthier goals. Maturing teens can learn this principle of delayed pleasure, rather than acting on instant gratification.

Hormones and curiosity are internal influences on teens' sexual interests. The remaining influences are external.

Influence #2: Media Messages

Today's culture sends messages every day about how to live life. The second influence that encourages sexual activity among teens involves a media that portrays a sexually active culture.

Let's start with today's movies. A recent Federal Trade Commission (FTC) study found that 80 percent of R-rated movies were targeting children under the age of 17. In fact, the FTC learned that two-thirds of the marketing plans for these movies expressly were aimed at those

3

under 17. A follow-up report by the Senate Commerce Committee revealed that the motion picture industry had cleaned up its advertising to teens in magazines and movie trailers, but ads for R-rated movies continue to appear on teens' most popular television programs.[7] Check out the plots of these R-rated films that drew large teen audiences.

• Four high school boys compete to be the first to lose their virginity by the time they go to college.[8]

• A young man tries to recover a videotape of a sexual encounter between a young woman who is not his girlfriend and him.[9]

• After breaking up with his girlfriend, a young man has numerous sexual encounters, finally trying to live without sex for a period of time.[10]

• Two people, needing companionship, come together in several sexually explicit scenes that portray both male and female nudity.[11]

What is the recurring message from these movies? That sex outside of marriage happens as a natural part of life; it's normal, fun, exciting and has no consequences.

Television programming fares no better. The sexual content on television programs rose from 56 to 68 percent over only five TV seasons, according to a study by the Kaiser Family Foundation. Made-for-TV movies contain the most sexual content (89 percent), followed by sitcoms at 84 percent and soap operas at 80 percent.[12] Three out of four 15- to 17-year-olds say that the sexual content on TV does affect the behavior of their friends.[13]

An average of 3.2 TV scenes per hour involve sexual messages. Since teens watch about 20 hours of TV a week, that exposure adds up.[14] Of all TV shows, nine percent involve teen characters who are sexually active.[15] The following plot lines come from popular TV shows teens watch.

• One girl tells everyone that she is pregnant from her one-night stand with a guy. Her friend, who also has slept with the same guy, tries to take the news in stride. The lead actress in this series remarked in a *seventeen* magazine interview, "I've had a lot more experiences than [my character] has. But she's getting more [experiences]. Now she's drinking and having sex." [16]

• *USA Today* has called this TV series "a one-hour ride on the Raging Teen-Hormone Express." *Entertainment Weekly* says this program was "the frankest depiction of teenage sexuality ever seen on the small screen." The teens on the show regularly discuss intercourse, homosexuality, and masturbation, as well as their different sexual couplings. [17]

• This highly popular comedy explores the social and sexual lives of four young women in New York City.

• MTV has had an impact on sex in programming and advertising during its 20 years on the air. Its music videos focus on teenagers between the ages of 12 and 19 years. Three-quarters of today's teens watch this channel an average of more than six hours a week. [18] Typically popular shows include: *Undressed,* in which group sex and teen sex are highlighted; the reality-based *The Real World* and *Road Rules,* in which an unusual amount of sex is discussed and flaunted; and the cancelled *Jackass* (which continues in reruns) where one show features a "spermathon" showing cast members masturbating. In addition, 75 percent of the music videos tell a story that involves sexual imagery. [19]

Like films, television blatantly portrays the message that sex outside of marriage is natural, normal, fun, exciting and has no consequences.

Music creates another media influence on teens. Many teens form their ideas about relationships based on the music they hear. According to a Federal Trade Commission's report, 85 percent of the 13- to 16-year-olds who participated in the study purchased music with explicit lyrics that was rated for 17-year-olds and older. [20] A House of Representatives Subcommittee follow-up study found that the music industry did nothing to change those statistics. The five major recording companies continued to place advertising for explicit content music on television programs that young teens watch.[21] For those of us who normally do not shop in the teen music area, here's just one example of a popular lyric:

- "So kids say no to drugs – smoke crack . . . so don't do drugs – suck my motherf___ing penis – so there'll be more for me." (Eminem, *The Kids*)

What is the recurring message? Anything goes – the more extreme, the better. Women are here to be used – and besides, women really like it that way.

Finally, the Internet, a valuable tool for finding information and staying connected with others, has a dark side. Several studies report that seven out of ten teens have a computer at home, and anywhere from one-half to three-quarters of these have Internet access. By comparison, only 56 percent of today's adults are online.[22] By simply punching the letters S•E•X into a search engine on the Web, youth can find every kind of explicit sex in graphic pictures without ever having to give a credit card number. Anyone searching on the Web can find descriptions of sites that are almost pornographic in their explanations. These Web sites specialize in shock, titillation, and the outrageous. They not only are blatant in form, but offer a very unrealistic view of sex. Today's Web has become the *Playboy* magazine for this generation of youth with two main differences - it can be accessed easily, and it is infinitely more explicit. And, unlike *Playboy*, it often may come into the home uninvited.

Other areas of the Internet that often are overlooked, but are enjoyed by teenagers, are chat rooms. In some chat rooms, teens can take on older identities, use descriptive, foul language, and participate in cybersex with other chat room participants. Not all chat rooms are pornographic. Some function under the pretext of helping teens with their questions about sexuality. These chat rooms are dangerous, because they may share values that are different from those you hope your teen will develop. They appear acceptable on the surface, but their message is to help teens have sex.

The recurring message from these Web sites and chat rooms is that sexual images and ideas are acceptable fantasies for the mind. Sixty million people use the Internet. It is estimated that 2 million of these are sexually addicted Internet users. The Internet becomes a dangerous place for addiction because it offers isolation, fantasy, anonymity and sexual images.[23]

Influence #3: Peer Pressure

Hormones and curiosity create inner pressures on teens. The media is an example of an external influence on teens. Another external influence takes the form of peers who apply pressure to their friends to become sexually active.

How long do you think it takes before the talk in the guys' locker room turns to sex? The questions and comparisons can be brutal. Many boys believe that having sex is a rite of passage necessary to become a man. Guys are two times more likely than girls to expect sex in a relationship. In fact, they often let a girl's prior sexual experience determine their decisions about sex.[24] And, while most teen boys say they think love and marriage are important reasons for waiting, boys who have been sexually active state that opportunity was what led to their first sexual experience.[25]

Peer pressure doesn't happen just among boys. Due to the recent rise of sexual awareness among females, girls have their own version of locker room talk that can be aggressive and even graphic. What's the number one topic at any all-girl spend-the-night party? Guys, of course. The subject soon evolves into a discussion of sex. These girls comfortably talk about the topic of sex because they see it openly discussed on their favorite TV shows.

Influence #4: Alcohol

Another strong influence on teens becoming sexually active involves the use and abuse of alcohol by teens. Here are the facts:

• Teens 15 and older who drink alcohol are seven times more likely to have sex than those who don't.[26]
• Those who drink are also more likely to have several sexual partners.[27]

Since alcohol is a depressant, it suppresses a teen's normal inhibitions. Even if a teen has a strong commitment to sexual abstinence, drinking lowers that teen's ability to think correctly and remember personal goals. Drinking also opens up a teen to other at-risk behaviors, such as doing drugs, smoking, vandalism, and violence.

Unfortunately, many teens who drink are binge drinkers. Binge drinking is defined as the consumption of more than four (for girls) or five (for boys) drinks in one sitting. A national survey revealed that 51 percent of high school seniors, 40 percent of 10th-graders, and 24 percent of eighth-graders use alcohol each month. Of these, a third of the seniors, 25 percent of the 10th-graders, and 15 percent of the eighth-graders binge drink regularly.[28]

Influence #5: Relationship Pressure

The final influence is the perceived idea that sex is an expected part of a meaningful relationship. After all, isn't that what happens in the movies and on television? A guy meets a girl. There's chemistry between them, they fall in love, then they fall into bed.

Boys and girls view sex in different ways. Guys can separate the physical act of sex from a personal relationship. They can use sex as a physical release with minimal emotional bonding. Girls, however tend to see sex as a part of a larger emotional relationship with the other person.[29] Girls may use sex to build relationships. In other words, boys can use love to get sex, and girls can use sex to get love. For both sexes, emotional and physical relationships grow more intense due to hormonal changes. How does this play out in real life?

Let's follow a typical teenage girl on a date with her boyfriend of six months. After a school dance, the couple goes to a party at a friend's house. Some time during the party they wander to an isolated spot in the backyard. They start kissing. The boy tells the girl that he loves her. She responds in the same way to him. Then he challenges her. "If you really love me, prove it. Let's show our love to each other in a real way," as he continues to kiss and stroke her. Here's the girl's dilemma: She doesn't want to lose her boyfriend, especially if she feels this tingly kind of chemistry with him. But, is it necessary to have sex to keep the relationship? Most teens who develop meaningful romantic relationships eventually struggle with the decision to act out their love in a sexual way. In fact, 51 percent of the sexually active 15- to 17-year-olds said the major reason they had sex the first time was that they thought they had met the right person. That was followed closely by 45 percent who first had sex because the other person wanted to.[30]

Teens fail to realize the difference between the intensity of sexual feelings and real love. Sex can be a physical act detached from any real commitment. In a loving relationship, you commit to caring for another person, instead of yourself. Romantic love goes beyond feelings and is strong enough to withstand different situations and circumstances over a period of time. Too often teens confuse the intensity of sex with the intimacy of love. Even adults can get caught in the trap of substituting intensity for intimacy.

But Everyone Is NOT Doing IT!

Every teen worries about not fitting in, about being rejected by his or her peers. Imagine the internal struggle of teens who constantly hear "Everyone's doing it. What's wrong with you?" The facts, however, show that everyone is *not* doing it.

- More than 50 percent of today's teens have not had sexual intercourse.[31]
- Only one-third of the previously sexually active teens had had sex in the past three months.[32]
- Half the teens who could have participated in sexual intercourse with someone they liked decided against it.[33]

There is Hope

And the hope comes directly from teens themselves. One hundred teens were interviewed for this book. All of the teens who participated in the survey have chosen to be abstinent until marriage. Throughout the book, look for their honest, expressive ideas. These teens tell us there is hope, but the solution is multi-faceted, not simplistic. Their answers provide the basis for the 10 proven steps you as a parent can take to help your teen commit to abstinence until marriage. You have taken the first step by becoming informed. (To review a copy of the survey, see Appendix A.)

Parent: Let's Think About It!

Rate yourself to see how well you know your teen and the influences in his or her life. Use this scale of one to five:

1   It's never occurred to me to do this.
2   I've thought about it.
3   I tried, but got no response from my teen.
4   I've done this once.
5   I do this often.

_____ 1. I discuss the physical and emotional changes happening in my teen's life, including the strange and strong sexual urges.

_____ 2. I know the message and content of the movies that my teen watches.

_____ 3. I watch a movie (in the theater or on video) with my teen and discuss the sexual content.

_____ 4. I watch my teen's favorite TV programs, and talk with my teen about the reality of sex and relationships, as depicted on the show.

_____ 5. I listen to (or read) the lyrics of several of the CDs my teen purchases and/or listens to, and I know the sexual messages being presented.

_____ 6. I monitor my teen's use of the computer, including the sites he or she visits on the Internet.

_____ 7. I discuss the dangers of Internet chat rooms with my teen.

_____ 8. I know the names and situations of the friends with whom my teen hangs out.

_____ 9. I talk with my teen about the dangers of alcohol, especially in sexual situations.

_____ 10. I talk with my teen about dating and how to handle unwanted sexual situations.

Add up your score. If you have 45 to 50 points, you are either kidding yourself or you have excellent communication with your teen. If you have 38 to 44 points, you are trying to stay in touch with your teen, but can use some help; keep reading! If you have 30 to 37 points, you are struggling, but will find the exercises in this book helpful in getting your teen to talk. If you have 29 or fewer points, don't despair. At least you are making an effort by reading this book. Keep looking for ways to make these things happen.

Parent and Teen: Let's Talk About It!
Discussion One – "Everybody's Talking About It!"

1. **The Debate.** The following teens are discussing sex. Read the teens' statements, then discuss the questions below.

Steve: *"You see sex everywhere, in the movies, on advertisements, in magazines, on the Internet. I'm young and want to enjoy all there is in life. If I see a good-looking girl, I'm attracted to her body. I think most everybody in school is having sex; most of my friends are. It's not a big deal like it used to be, and I certainly don't want to be left out. If you find someone you care about, and that girl wants to do it, then I don't see anything wrong with it. If you're careful, nothing can really go wrong."*

Tony: *"To me there are too many risks involved with sex. The risk of teen pregnancy and getting a sexually transmitted disease seem too great. Plus, there are things I want to do with my life. I want to play sports and go to college, and I'm not willing to risk all that. I also think when you sleep with somebody you give a little of yourself away. After a while, you don't care about yourself. I think you should save yourself for the person you're willing to spend your life with. You can still love someone and show your love without having to have sex. I remain abstinent and plan on keeping my virginity until I get married. A lot of people I know are not having sex. I hear a lot more of 'Cool, you're a virgin,' you know."*

◆ How would you describe Steve's view of sex?

◆ How would you describe Tony's view of sex?

◆ How do you feel about having sex before marriage?

• Teen's view _____

• Parent's view _____

2. **Did You Know?** Read each statement below. Circle **T** if you think the statement is true and **F** if you think the statement is false. Look up the answers at the end of this section and compare them with your responses.

T   F   1. The majority of teens today are not having sex.[1]

T   F   2. One out of every four sexually active teens will contract an STD (sexually transmitted disease).[2]

T   F   3. Teens do not have to worry about contracting HIV/AIDS.

T   F   4. One out of every 20 girls will become pregnant by the age of 18.

T   F   5. Sexually active girls are nearly three times more likely to attempt suicide than girls who are virgins.[3]

3. **Movies and SEX.** Read the following themes from several popular movies. What is the message that these movies make about sex? Do you agree or disagree with that message? Support your ideas.

♦ Four high school boys compete to be the first to lose their virginity by the time they go to college.[4]

♦ A young man tries to recover a videotape of a sexual encounter between him and a young woman who is not his girlfriend.

♦ After breaking up with his girlfriend, a young man has numerous sexual encounters, finally trying to live without sex for a period of time.

♦ Two people, needing companionship, come together in several sexually explicit scenes that portray both male and female nudity.

Movie Messages _____

_____

❏ Agree
❏ Disagree

4. **Alcohol and SEX.** Read these real-life accounts of how alcohol has affected these teens, and discuss the questions following the stories.

Tasha: *"I am extremely vulnerable when I drink alcohol. While I was at several parties, I drank too much, got involved with some guys, and ended up having sex with several guys I hardly knew. At one party I got drunk, and the guy I was with raped me."* [5]

> **Darin:** *"Alcohol has definitely caused me to make some bad decisions. When I'm with girls and alcohol is involved, I really lack self-control. I used to party a lot and go to parties on weekends and get drunk and do whatever and not remember what happened the next day."* [6]

Farrah: *"It can be a bad situation when you're high and you don't really know what you're saying and what you're doing and you can't control yourself. You know what you're doing, but you can't control what you're doing all the time."* [7]

♦ How did alcohol affect these teens?

♦ What were the consequences of mixing alcohol and sex?

5. **What Do You Know?** Read each statement below. Circle **T** if you think the statement is true and **F** if you think the statement is false. Look up the answers at the end of this section and compare them with your responses.

T	F	1. Alcohol is a drug because it chemically alters the way your body and mind work.
T	F	2. Alcohol is a stimulant that makes you feel better.
T	F	3. Alcohol speeds up brain development to make a young person think more like an adult.
T	F	4. Drinking large amounts of alcohol at one time can lead to death.
T	F	5. Alcohol helps you think more clearly.
T	F	6. There is more alcohol in a shot of liquor than in a

can of beer or a glass of wine.

T   F   7. Young drinkers can develop an addiction, or dependence, on alcohol.

T   F   8. Alcoholism is a disease, and while it is treatable, there is no known cure.

T   F   9. Alcohol helps social development, so you become more friendly and fun.

Answers to Did You Know?: 1-T; 2-T; 3-F (The CDC estimates that about half of all new HIV infections are among young people under the age of 25.[8]); 4-F (One out of five sexually active girls becomes pregnant by age 18.[9]); 5-T.

Answers to Alcohol quiz: 1-T; 2-F (Alcohol is a depressant.); 3-F (Alcohol slows down brain development.); 4-T; 5-F; 6-F (It's the same amount.); 7-T; 8-T; 9-F (Alcohol slows down social development.)

2

Step Two

Explain the Risks

What They Don't Know Can Kill Them

What Are the Risks?

In the world of sexual activity, few talk about the risks – neither the media nor their peers, not the "safe-sex" advocates, and sometimes, not even parents. But what we don't tell teens can destroy their futures, the futures of others, and in some cases it might even kill them.

- One quarter of all new cases of sexually transmitted diseases occurs in teens. That's 4 million teens each year who contract an STD.[1]
- By the age of 18, 20 percent of all sexually active girls will have been pregnant.[2]
- With 820,000 girls getting pregnant each year, that averages 2,300 teenagers who become pregnant each day![3]
- Half of all new HIV infections are among young people under the age of 25.[4]
- There are no statistics to measure the broken hearts, the misplaced trust, and damaged emotions resulting from teen sexual activity.

Don't you want to do everything possible to guarantee that your teenager clearly understands the real dangers of premarital sex? Are you interested in eliminating behaviors that place your teen at risk? Let's examine these risks. Some risks are obvious; others are more subtle. Some you may know about; others may surprise you. The risks are grouped into three categories: emotional risks, pregnancy risk, and disease risks.

The Emotional Risks

One of the most overlooked risks of sexual activity involves the teen's emotions. Feelings are not only hard to measure, but they also get mixed in with the already volatile emotions of the teen years. Unless parents take time to remember their own roller coaster emotions as a teen, they may forget that a teen's emotions are raw and vulnerable. Sexual activity adds to that confusion. Often teens suffer emotional pain alone, keeping it inside because they don't know how to talk about it. See how devastating the emotional risks are, as these young people describe the emotional impact of sexual activity on their lives.

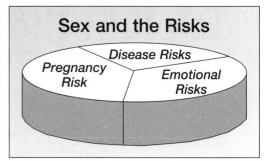

"There are a lot of emotional and inner consequences I'm suffering through." (9th-grade girl)[5]

"The first time I had sex, I have never felt worse. I've never felt more scared in my life." (12th-grade boy)[6]

"I think I've been emotionally affected in a lot of ways. I struggle with a lot of guilt and loneliness . . . I don't have any friends." (12th-grade girl)[7]

"I've lived with the disappointment of knowing that I had a really cool destiny and that I let it go." (Adult who became a teen mother)[8]

"It's been very, very hard. I have to see a counselor now and that's something I never thought I'd do or be caught doing. Everyone wants to live an ideal life . . . like a fairytale. But once I put myself in the position that I have, it's more of a nightmare than a fantasy." (Teen mother)[9]

"Sex before marriage for me meant that I would never know if a guy really loved me. I would never know what it meant to be chosen, and not lusted after . . . and the difference between those two has haunted me for my entire life." (Young adult woman)[10]

What emotional effects did you notice in the comments of these young adults and teens? Here are some emotional consequences that can concern sexually-active teens.

- **Worry** – What if someone finds out? What if I get pregnant (or get someone else pregnant)? What if my parents find out? Did I contract a sexually transmitted disease? What if my boyfriend tells his friends?
- **Guilt** – Why did I do something I didn't want to do? Do my actions go against my morals? How do my actions fit in with my personal convictions and my goals? Why did I go against my parents' expectations for me? Did I use him or her for my sexual needs? Why did I give myself away so easily?
- **Fear of Future Relationships** – Now that I've shown him I love him, will he leave me? How do I know whom to trust? Will my next girlfriend expect sex, too? Is she just interested in my body for sex, or does she care about me as a person? Why do I keep doing this over and over?

> **The Rose**
>
> In *Choosing the Best PATH*, an abstinence curriculum for middle school students, the leader uses a rose to demonstrate the emotional consequences. The leader passes around a rose and asks each student to take a petal before passing it on. When the stem returns to the leader, the rose is ruined. This visual demonstration helps students see how a person gives away part of himself or herself through casual sex. This lowers a person's feelings of self-worth. Often someone with a low self-esteem will participate in other self-defeating behaviors, such as drinking alcohol, taking drugs, or becoming sexually promiscuous.

- **Loss of Self-Respect** – Why do I feel like I've failed? Now that I have an STD, what guy is going to want me for a wife? Why do I feel like I brought it all on myself? Why do I hate the way others treat me?
- **Ruined Relationships** – Why is sex the center of our relationship? Can't we do other things like we did before we started having sex? Why is she so jealous of the time I spend with my buddies? Why does he get so violent when I don't feel like having sex?

The teen years create their own emotional turmoil. Hormonal changes, body growth, shifting relationships, startling new feelings, the desire for independence, the fear of being alone, the need to emotionally detach from the family, the desire to belong to someone, the need to learn self-control – all of these feelings define the experience of adolescence. Add sexual activity to the mix, and teens are primed for huge emotional pain.

Emotional Hurt

No wonder the emotions generated during sexual activity among teenagers may contribute to clinical depression, even suicide. Research studies indicate that girls who have sex are three times more likely to attempt suicide than girls who are virgins.[11] Sexually active guys are eight times more likely to attempt suicide than guys who are virgins.[12]

These emotional risks occur because sex is a part of life meant to be shared in an intimate, committed relationship. Giving this very personal part of life to someone without the commitment and emotional security of marriage devalues a person's feelings of worth. The person no longer feels secure in pursuing emotional intimacy.

This emotional baggage can carry over into adult life. A couple of the earlier comments in this section came from young adult women. Looking back on their lives, they expressed continual sadness for how their teenage sexual activity had robbed them of their teen years and continued to control their adult years. Among teens surveyed, 66 percent of all sexually active teens said they "wished they'd waited longer" to have sex.[13]

Can a condom protect against the broken hearts and these emotional consequences of teen sex? Of course not! Yet the emotional effects of teen sexual activity are just as real, and potentially devastating, as any other consequence. Only abstinence until marriage truly protects your teen's emotional well-being and health.

The Pregnancy Risk

Although the teen pregnancy rate has dropped in the last few years, 820,000 girls become pregnant each year.[14] That averages out to almost 2,300 teens who become pregnant each day! By the age of 18, one in five sexually active girls will have been pregnant.[15]

Teen pregnancy often results in spiraling consequences for the teen mother, the baby, and the teen father. Usually teens are unprepared emotionally and financially to take care of a baby, as well as themselves. Look at how this real-life teen couple struggled through the trauma of a teen pregnancy. Their names are Raoul and Nicole,[16] but they could be Jim and Mary, Rasmond and Autumn, Jorge and Gena. Their story is familiar.

At 14, Nicole didn't think she could get pregnant. Raoul was 17. Both found it hard to believe that they were going to be parents. Nicole shared her feelings about being a pregnant teen:

"I feel like I've let myself down, in a way, because now I know I don't have as much going for me as I probably could've without a baby."

- Less than one-third of teen mothers ever earn a high school diploma.[17]
- Guys who father a child as an adolescent average just over 11 years of education.[18]
- Teen mothers are more likely to face poverty and single parenthood.[19]
- Teen mothers are more likely to have children with low birth weight and related health problems.[20]
- Children of teen parents are more likely to drop out of school than those born to adult parents.[21]

Raoul thought about dropping out of school so he could work to support Nicole and the baby. If he did, he would be working in a minimum wage job. He was surprised at how hard it was to get a job without a high school diploma.

Unlike many teen fathers, Raoul told Nicole that he wanted to be a part of the baby's life, although they did not plan to be married. Many teen fathers do not bear any responsibility for fathering a child.

After 12 hours of painful labor, Nicole delivered a girl. Raoul expressed concern during the delivery:

"I'm worried about the baby, if it's gonna come out OK, or if it's gonna be sick."

Raoul and Nicole's baby girl Emily was born without any birth defects. What the young couple didn't realize was that following her birth the real commitment began. Nicole described what she faces each day:

"Her crying, her always wanting to eat. You know I can't really get a lot of things done around the house. My teen years were [tiny]."

After the baby's birth, Raoul continued to look for a job, without much success. He came over to see Nicole and Emily when he could, but his visits weren't always pleasant. He reflected:

"Now that the baby's here, there's more arguing between me and Nicole. Now it's about the baby, not about us. I don't even wanna have sex 'cause I mean, I don't wanna make another baby."

Nicole is determined to give Emily a better life than she chose:

"I definitely don't wanna see her get pregnant at 14. I don't want her to end up like I did."

Despite what many believe, condoms don't eliminate the risk of a teen pregnancy. They break and slip off, and it's hard to get teens to use them correctly and consistently. This 18-year-old teen father tells what happened when the condom broke.

"Back when I was 15 I became a daddy. At 14 I found out. Just one day, the condom busted. Man, I just had a feeling. And the thoughts

running through my head of leaving, you know, splitting. We didn't talk about abortion. We didn't talk about adoption. I guess we just accepted that she was having a baby and that was it.

"When my little boy was about a year and a half his mom left... My friends call up, 'Hey, wanna go cruising?' I say, 'Hey, got room for a car seat?'

"This is my life 24-7. I can't take him back and say you know what, I don't want him no more, here. All sales are final."[22]

The Disease Risks – STDs (Sexually Transmitted Diseases)

Forty years ago there were two sexually transmitted diseases, then called venereal diseases. They were gonorrhea and syphilis – both curable by penicillin. Currently, there are more than 25 sexually transmitted diseases – some are incurable; others lead to death.[23] The statistics involving teens are staggering:

- There are 15 million new sexually transmitted disease (STD) cases each year in the United States.[24] Of those, 4 million teenagers get a sexually transmitted disease each year, or one teen acquires an STD every eight seconds.[25]
- Approximately one in four sexually active teens contracts an STD each year.[26]
- Most sexually active teens have never talked about STDs with anyone in health care, and 70 percent have never been tested.[27]
- Many don't know, or don't accept, that infertility and cancer can result from an STD.[28]
- Many teens believe that participating in oral sex protects them from STDs. Health officials report that STDs are being passed through oral sex.[29]

There are two kinds of STDs – bacterial, which are treatable, and viral, which have no cure. Let's look at the STDs that are most prevalent among teens. You can see examples of the effects of these STDs by turning to Appendix B in the back of the book.

One of the most common bacterial STDs in the United States is

chlamydia. More than 3 million new cases are diagnosed each year,[30] including 1.5 million young people aged 15-24.[31] Chlamydia produces very few visible symptoms, so a teenager may not realize he or she is infected. In fact, up to 75 percent of the chlamydia infections in women have no symptoms. That number drops to 50 percent for men.[32] Common symptoms, if present, include abnormal discharges or a burning sensation while urinating. In Appendix B, Figure 1 shows a healthy cervix. Figure 2 shows what chlamydia can do to a cervix.

Chlamydia is diagnosed by lab tests and can be cured with antibiotics. However, because of the lack of symptoms, chlamydia often is not diagnosed early enough to keep it from causing complications. Left untreated in women, chlamydia can lead to pelvic inflammatory disease (PID). The tubular damage caused by PID can result in infertility in women of childbearing age. PID also can cause intense pelvic pain. Any damage done by chlamydia cannot be reversed. Figure 3 in Appendix B shows the damage of PID. Increasing numbers of women get married and are ready to start a family when they learn they are infertile because of PID.

A female has a 50 percent chance of getting **gonorrhea** from a single act of sex with an infected partner.[33] Although new cases of gonorrhea have declined in the last 20 years, rates continue to rise among teens and ethnic minorities.[34] Because of a developing cervix, teenage girls are more susceptible to cervical infections like chlamydia and gonorrhea than more mature women.[35] Like chlamydia, untreated gonorrhea can result in PID, which is irreversible. Some strains of gonorrhea are resistant to penicillin, which was used in the past. Combinations of antibiotics are used to treat this bacterial infection.[36]

The most common viral STD is the **human papillomavirus or HPV**. With 5.5 million cases each year, this is the fastest growing STD in the United States.[37] Over 30 types of HPV can affect the genital area. Some strains of HPV can produce genital warts, which are small growths on the outside or inside of the genital area. Figures 4 and 5 in Appendix B show examples of a male and a female with genital warts. Genital warts may be removed through various treatments including acid, freezing or surgery. However, in some cases, genital warts continue to come back, even after treatment. Some types of HPV can also cause cervical cancer. Cervical cancer kills nearly 4,000 women a year in the United States.[38] Like other STDs, HPV usually causes an infection with no noticeable symptoms. The disease can be spread by sexual contact without either partner realizing it. It may show up later when other problems occur. Because HPV is a virus there is no cure. It's up to the body's immune system to fight off the infection. Sometimes this occurs within a few weeks, months, or even years. In some cases it remains for life. The HPV strains that last the longest are the most likely to cause cervical cancer.[39] Regular Pap tests, performed by a doctor, are important for detecting cervical cancer early, when it can be treated most effectively.

With 1 million new cases a year, **genital herpes** is the second most common viral STD.[40] Currently, there are 45 million cases of genital herpes in the United States,[41] or one in every five Americans over the age of 12.[42] Blisters usually appear in and around the vaginal area, on the penis, around the anus, or on the hips and thighs. Blisters can also appear on other skin surfaces where broken skin has come in contact with the virus. Blisters indicate the virus is active; but even when there are no blisters, the virus can be passed through sexual contact. Figures 6 and 7 in Appendix B show a male and a female with genital herpes.

In Appendix B, Figure 8 illustrates how genital herpes works in the body. After a blister forms, it will open and "weep" until it dries up. Then, the virus moves along the nerve cells and lodges near the spine. Any kind of stress can bring the virus back to the surface where it again forms blisters. Because this is a virus, there is no cure.

The HIV/AIDS Risk

In 1981, there were 31 cases of AIDS. After 20 years, AIDS has killed more than 20 million people, and another 39.4 million are currently living with HIV/AIDS worldwide.[43] Over 1 million people in the United States are living with HIV/AIDS and about one quarter do not know they are infected.[44] Each year over 40,000 new cases of HIV/AIDS are diagnosed in the United States.[45] Additional evidence shows that those with other STDs are two to five times more likely to contract the HIV infection.[46] Because the AIDS virus destroys the body's ability to fight off infections, those with AIDS are susceptible to numerous other diseases, including cancer. HIV/AIDS can only be contracted through sexual transmission, shared infected needles, blood transfusions received from someone with AIDS, or passed from a mother to a child at birth. Sexual transmission can also occur through oral sex.

As you've read about the three risks of teen sexual activity – emotional risks, pregnancy risk, and disease risks – have you wondered what you can do to protect your teen? In the next Step, you will see that condoms do not fully protect your teen, not from pregnancy, nor from STDs. You know you can't be a 24/7 bodyguard to your teen. The only way to help your teens eliminate these risks from their lives is to encourage them to choose abstinence until marriage. It begins by helping your teen understand the risks.

Parent: Let's Think About It!

1. What risk was most surprising to you? Why?

    _____ emotional   _____ pregnancy
    _____ STDs   _____ HIV/AIDS

2. What other emotions besides worry, guilt, fear of future relationships, loss of self-respect, and ruined relationships do you think sexually active teens face?

3. What did you learn about the teen pregnancy risk?

4. How is a teen pregnancy a risk to the father? How is a teen pregnancy a risk to the baby?

5. Before reading the section about STDs, what STDs could you name?

    _____   _____   _____

    _____   _____

6. What did you learn about STDs that you want to share with your teen?

7. What are some other sexual risks that weren't mentioned that you want to discuss with your teen?

Parent and Teen: Let's Talk About It!
Discussion Two – Understanding the Risks

There are three major risks for teens who are sexually active: emotional risks, pregnancy risk, and disease risks – STDs.

1. **Emotional Risks.** Read these comments from real-life teens, then discuss the questions below.

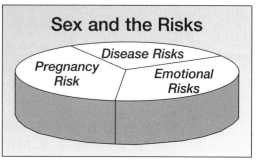

Sex and the Risks

Disease Risks

Pregnancy Risk

Emotional Risks

John *(10th-grade): "I didn't know about the emotional side of sex. I don't think a lot of teens know about it. I didn't know about it until I lost my virginity, and it was devastating. The first time I had sex, I have never felt worse. I've never felt more scared in my life"* [1]

Julia *(12th-grade): "I think I have been emotionally affected in a lot of ways. I struggle with a lot of guilt and loneliness. Whether you like it or not, there are emotional bonds that develop when you have sex. I see a counselor now and that's something I never thought I'd do or be caught dead doing."* [2]

◆ What are some of the emotional consequences John and Julia experienced?

◆ How does being sexually active as a teen affect how a person might feel about himself or herself?

◆ Why do you think sexually active girls are nearly three times more likely to attempt suicide than girls who are virgins? [3]

◆ Why do you think sexually active guys are eight times more likely to attempt suicide than guys who are virgins? [4]

2. **Pregnancy Risk**. Read what these real-life teens say about teen pregnancy. Then discuss the questions.

Sharon (young mother): *"Looking back, my teen years were so short. I believe I was very naive and actually really dumb for thinking that I wasn't going to get pregnant. I got sick a lot during my pregnancy because of my age. I wish that I could have finished school and graduated and perhaps gone to college. My daughter was a year-and-a-half when her father and I broke up. He said he would always be there, but now the only time I see him is in court, when the support payments are late."*

Marco (young father): *"Back when I was 15, I became a daddy. At 14 I found out. Just one day, the condom busted. Man, I just had a feeling. And the thought's running through my head of leaving, you know, splitting. We didn't talk about abortion. We didn't talk about adoption. I guess we just accepted that she was having a baby and that was it.*

"When my little boy was about a year and a half his mom left . . . My friends call up, 'Hey, wanna go cruising?' I say, 'Hey, got room for a car seat?'

"This is my life 24-7. I can't take him back and say you know what, I don't want him no more, here. All sales are final." [5]

◆ Why did these teens think they wouldn't get pregnant?

◆ How did their lives change after they got pregnant?

◆ **Teen:** How would an unplanned pregnancy affect your life?

3. **Disease Risks – STDs.** In the following real-life stories you'll learn about young people who contracted STDs. After each story is a brief description of the STD. Discuss the questions at the end of this section.

In Appendix B are a set of pictures that will help you understand what these STDs look like and what they can do.

◆ **Chlamydia:** *"The first time I had sex with anybody, I got chlamydia. So one week I was a virgin, and two weeks later I had an STD."* [6]

"I became violently ill. I had a 105 fever, severe, abdominal cramps, and throwing up. The conclusion was I was infertile. My tubes had been damaged beyond repair." [7]

> *About Chlamydia*
> • This is one of the most common *bacterial* STDs in the United States, with 3 million new cases reported every year. [8]
> • Chlamydia often produces no symptoms, but when it does, they might include abnormal discharges or a burning sensation while urinating.
> • Chlamydia can be diagnosed by lab tests; it can be cured by antibiotics.
> • **Problem**: There are often no symptoms, and if chlamydia is left untreated, it can lead to pelvic inflammatory disease (PID). PID can cause damage to the reproductive organs causing infertility and intense pelvic pain. Any damage to internal organs is permanent; it cannot be reversed.

Figure 1 in Appendix B is of a woman's healthy cervix. The cervix is the opening at the top of the vagina. Figure 2 shows a cervix that is inflamed with chlamydia. The infection makes the woman's cervix red and swollen. It bleeds easily when touched. Pus can be seen in the center dripping from the cervix. The woman got this infection from sexual intercourse with a man who was infected with chlamydia who had no symptoms.

Figure 3 in the Appendix is a picture of a woman in her late 20's. She has scarring in her fallopian tubes from chlamydia. Her uterus, fallopian tubes, and ovaries are shiny white, and about the size and color of new golf balls. At the end of the left fallopian tube is a blue, ball-shaped object that is actually scar tissue, which has blocked the tube. Because of this blocked fallopian tube, she cannot have children.

◆ **Gonorrhea:** *"I was rushed to the hospital with intense abdominal pain. Emergency surgery revealed such a huge infection that my uterus, tubes, and ovaries all had to be removed. My husband of six months had infected me with gonorrhea, which he had contracted from a "one–night stand" prior to our engagement. Our dreams of biological children will never be realized."*

About Gonorrhea

• This is a common bacterial STD with an estimated 650,000 new cases occurring annually.[9] Gonorrhea is extremely infectious. A girl has a 50 percent chance of getting gonorrhea from a single encounter.[10]

• Many people have no initial symptoms. When symptoms do appear in a male they may include a painful, burning sensation when urinating and a pus-laden discharge from the urethra. For females, there may be a slight discharge, but most women have no symptoms.

• Gonorrhea can be treated and cured with antibiotics. But, like chlamydia, any damage done from untreated disease is irreversible.

◆ **Human Papillomavirus (HPV):** *"I was a sophomore in college. And it was somebody that I didn't know very well. I had had an abnormal pap a few months before I noticed the bumps that had not been there before. There was a lot of shame."* [11]

About HPV

• HPV is one of the most common viral STDs with more than 20 million people currently infected in the United States. There are 5.5 million new infections occurring every year.[12]

• HPV can cause genital warts and cervical cancer that kills nearly 4,000 women each year in the U.S.[13]

• HPV can be spread by skin-to-skin contact with the genital area of an infected partner. People can be infected with HPV and have no symptoms. Because HPV is a virus there is no cure. It's up to the body's immune system to fight off the infection.

Sometimes this occurs within a few weeks, months, or even years. In some cases it remains for life. The HPV strains that last the longest are the most likely to cause cervical cancer.[14]

In Appendix B, there are two pictures of genital warts caused by HPV. In Figure 4 the genital warts are on a man's penis. In many cases the warts can be so small they are undetectable. In Figure 5 there is a small genital wart on the outside genital area of a woman.

♦ **Genital Herpes:** *"We'd done the right things. We'd been in a monogamous relationship. It didn't seem possible that I could have herpes. After an experience with oral sex, I noticed red bumps and had a fever. The open sore felt like someone was pouring lemon juice into an open cut. It was very painful. It never entered my mind that this could have happened through oral sex."* [15]

About Genital Herpes
• In the U.S. more than 45 million people are infected with genital herpes, about one in five over the age of 12. Over 1 million new infections occur every year.[16]
• Genital herpes produces blisters in and around the vaginal area, on the penis, around the anus, on the hips and thighs.
• Even when there is no blister, the virus can be passed through sexual contact. Because this is a virus, there is no cure.

In Appendix B, Figure 6 shows a herpes lesion on the underside of a man's penis. In Figure 7 you can see the herpes lesions on a woman's labia.

To understand how genital herpes works, look at Figure 8 in the Appendix. The picture shows how genital herpes attacks the body. After the initial blister opens and "weeps," it will dry up. Then the virus moves along the nerve cells and lodges near the spine. Any kind of stress can bring the virus back to the surface where it again forms blisters.

♦ **HIV/AIDS:** *"I'm 23 and I'm living with the AIDS virus. I contracted this disease at age 16. When I found out, it was during a routine check–up. I didn't know of anyone who was HIV positive that I slept with. They didn't look sick. I felt like this couldn't happen to me."*

About HIV/AIDS

• In 1981, there were 31 cases of AIDS. After 20 years, AIDS has killed more than 20 million people, and another 39.4 million are currently living with HIV/AIDS worldwide.[17] Over 1 million people in the U.S. are living with HIV/AIDS and about one quarter do not know they are.[18] Each year more than 40,000 cases of HIV/AIDS are diagnosed in the U.S.[19]

• HIV (Human Immunodeficiency Virus) is a retrovirus that attacks the immune cells in the body. As it spreads through the cells, it damages the immune system. This leaves the person exposed to simple infections and diseases that normally would not be a problem.

• HIV/AIDS can only be contracted through sexual transmission (including oral sex), shared infected needles, receiving a blood transfusion from someone with HIV/AIDS, or passed from a mother to a child at birth. There is no cure for HIV/AIDS.

◆ Why did these young people think that the consequences of sex couldn't happen to them?

◆ How did contracting an STD change their lives?

◆ **Teen:** How would your life change if you contracted a sexually transmitted disease?

◆ What did you already know about STDs? What was new to you?

◆ What is the only sure way to eliminate the risk of contracting an STD?

Conclusion

What is the only way to totally eliminate the emotional risks, the pregnancy risk, and the disease risks?

_____

_____

_____

3

Step Three

Be Committed

Mixed Messages Don't Work

Dr. Freda McKissic Bush is a medical doctor of obstetrics and gynecology in Jackson, Mississippi. Professionally, Bush prescribed birth control and handed out condoms to sexually active patients. She was quick to admit that she had some ambivalence about the total abstinence message. Personally, like many parents, her message to her three daughters and one son was to "remain abstinent until you are married – but if you can't, make sure you use a condom for protection."

When her oldest daughter, who was a college sophomore, took her to lunch and told Bush that she was pregnant, Bush states, "We knew we could no longer send 'mixed messages'. The time had come to communicate clearly that the standard for our family is that you save sex for marriage – period. When we pass out condoms, we compromise our children's lives. When we do nothing or think we can do nothing, we are complacent about [our children's] potential destruction." Bush and her husband realized that parents must be decisive, not only in the public health message to abstain from sex until marriage, but also decisive about abstinence as a lifestyle.

Bush saw the need not only to teach abstinence to her children, but also to raise the character issue – to have the courage to stand up for what is right, to develop a healthy respect for yourself and others, and to have the determination to make decisions to reach a goal. "This time we got it right," Dr. Bush explains. "Our children now hear a clear message from both their parents, and they see it modeled in self-control, honesty, and a life lived in integrity." Today, her oldest daughter is married. Her second daughter is committed to renewed virginity. Her two youngest children are in college, and are proud to be known as virgins. Today, both Dr. Bush and her husband are involved in teaching abstinence-until-marriage education in Jackson public schools and in after-school programs targeted for the African-American community.[1]

Dr. Bush's story represents the problem facing many parents. We want to direct our teens toward making wise, healthy, safe choices. We think we are giving direct messages, yet we complicate the message by offering unhealthy compromises. In reality, we mix up those messages.

Mixing Up the Messages

A mixed message contains two things that conflict with one another. Here are a few mixed messages we've all said:

- Be home by midnight, but if you can't, call and tell us where you are.
- Don't watch television until you finish your homework, but if you do, don't wait too late to get it done.
- Clean up your room before you go out, or at least make sure you get it done by Saturday.

What do teens hear in a mixed message? They have selective hearing just like we do. They hear the second part of the message, which is easier and least restrictive.

Now apply this mixed message philosophy to at-risk teen behaviors. These are behaviors that affect the lives and futures of our teens. Most parents wouldn't say:

- Don't drink and drive, but if you do, make sure you are in a large car with your seat belt firmly fastened.
- Don't smoke, but if you do, only smoke filtered cigarettes.
- Don't do drugs, but if you do, use clean needles.

We don't give these mixed messages, because we know teens hear only the less restrictive action in these at-risk behaviors. But, is it possible that some of us parents are sending a mixed message to our teens concerning at-risk sexual behavior?

The "Safe-Sex" Message

Ask any group of teens – even young teens – if they have heard of "safe sex" and nearly all of them have. The message of "safe sex" or "safer sex" has been stated a number of different ways by government health agencies and medical groups. Their message goes something like this:

- Condoms, if used consistently and correctly, are highly effective at preventing pregnancy and the transmission of STDs and HIV.
- Condoms are 98 percent effective in protecting against STDs and pregnancy, when used consistently and correctly.

The implication is clear – condoms are a way to protect yourself from the negative physical consequences of sex outside of marriage. (Notice there is no mention of the negative emotional consequences of a broken heart, feelings of guilt, or loss of self-esteem.)

While many parents do not want their teens to be sexually active, all parents certainly want to protect their teens from the devastating consequences of pregnancy, STDs, and HIV. Therefore, many well-intentioned parents believe the "safe-sex" message is acceptable. These parents tell their teenagers:

"I want you to be abstinent . . .
but if you are going to have sex, use protection."

How is this mixed message any different from the other at-risk mixed messages? What message do teens hear?

"It's OK to have sex."

Don't take my word for it. Here's what several teens (who did not choose to be abstinent until marriage) reported about their parents' expectations.

"They always told me that as long as I used protection, it was OK."

"As long as I used birth control, they really didn't care. They have condoms if I need them."

"Wait until you are 17."

"Think about it first; wait if you can, but if not, use protection."

"Use condoms, diaphragms, birth control pills, and oral sex."

With these mixed messages, is it any surprise that not one of these teens indicated an intention to remain abstinent until marriage?

Parents and their messages do make a difference in teens' actions. This was confirmed in a National Longitudinal Study of Adolescent Health, called *Add Health*. The study found that teens in the eighth-grade through the 11th-grade delayed sexual activity if they believed their mothers disapproved of that behavior. However, if mom recommended specific methods of birth control, the young person felt there was less disapproval of sexual activity.[2]

So What About "Safe Sex"?

As I stood before a press conference presenting the abstinence message, I noticed a determined hand waving to catch the attention of the moderator. The local newspaper reporter stood, looked at me, and asked, "Isn't it unrealistic to expect that all teens are going to be abstinent? Wouldn't you want to tell the sexually active teen how to have 'safe sex' with a condom, rather than using no protection at all?" This question addresses the basics of the current debate on sex education in America.

On the surface, the "safe sex" (updated to the friendlier "safer sex") message sounds reasonable, much more broad-minded and tolerant than the message that teenagers be abstinent until marriage.

Advocated by Planned Parenthood and other public health agencies, the "safer-sex" message is expressed on its teen-friendly Web site, *Teenwire*:

> *"You can be abstinent when you're in a relationship, but it only works when both people agree to it, so keep talking about it together.*
>
> *"One day your relationship may change, and your decision to be abstinent may change, too. Just remember: when you don't want to be abstinent anymore, check out your other birth control options, and get the info on how to protect yourself from infection."* [3]

But let's consider the facts.

"Safe Sex" Oversells the Effectiveness of Condoms

Remember, here is the definition of the effectiveness of condoms from the "safe-sex" advocates:

> *"For birth control and disease-prevention purposes, condoms fully rock. Use them the right way and they're 98 percent effective in preventing pregnancy, and they're the only known way to keep you from getting deadly STDs other than complete abstinence."* [4]

Do condoms provide 98 percent protection against pregnancy and sexually transmitted diseases? Will teens who use condoms be protected? Let's examine the facts about this part of the "safe-sex" message.

Condoms and Pregnancy

Remember that condoms are thin sheaths of rubber, plastic, or lambskin. They can break and slip off. Condoms also are susceptible to the deteriorating effects of age, heat, cold, and pressure. Many teens keep condoms in a wallet, hip pocket, or glove compartment – places that encourage deterioration. Studies show condoms break and slip off 1-4 percent of the time.[5]

Under "perfect use" conditions, which means a condom is used correctly every single time, condoms fail to prevent pregnancy 2 percent of the time, per year.[6] However, what happens when condoms are used by real-life people in real-life situations? Under "typical use" conditions, which reflect how often condoms fail for the average person who does not always use condoms consistently and correctly, condoms fail 15 percent of the time, per year.[7] This means that typically, 15 percent of women using condoms for birth control become pregnant within a year.

Even a low annual risk of pregnancy implies a high cumulative risk of pregnancy during a lifetime of use.[8] Let's assume a well-intentioned parent wants her ninth-grader to avoid the negative effects of a pregnancy, so she encourages the teen to use a condom when having sex. Let's assume the teen follows the parent's expectations and uses condoms with "typical effectiveness" over the four years in high school. Medical experts tell us the condom failure rate over those four years would place the girl at **nearly a 50 percent** chance of becoming pregnant![9] So, what are couples – married or unmarried – called who use condoms for birth control? You guessed it – parents!

Condoms and Sexually Transmitted Diseases

Did you know that there are more than 25 sexually transmitted diseases? Some have no cure; others end in death. Does the 98 percent protection of condoms apply to sexually transmitted diseases?

In a 2001 ground-breaking study by the National Institutes of Health, a panel of 28 medical experts reviewed more than 138 peer-reviewed, published reports on the effectiveness of condoms in reducing the risk of STDs. The results were shocking! The results of this study and others have proven that the "98 percent effectiveness" does NOT apply to STDs. In fact, the CDC states that "condom use cannot guarantee absolute protection against any STD."[10]

Here's what the research shows – when used every time, condoms are:

• Most effective against HIV, reducing the risk by 85 percent versus not

using a condom at all. However, 15 percent of the risk remains for a life-threatening disease with no cure.[11]
• Approximately 50 percent effective in reducing the risk of STDs spread by body fluid, such as chlamydia, gonorrhea, and trichomoniasis. However, 50 percent of the risk remains.[12]
• Less effective in reducing the risk of STDs spread by skin-to-skin contact (eg., herpes, syphilis, etc.). Condoms offer no protection if the infection is located in an area not covered by a condom.[13]
• Not effective in reducing the risk for HPV, the most common viral STD. However, some risk reduction may occur with HPV-related symptoms (e.g. warts and cervical cancer).[14]

More than 15 million people acquire an STD in America each year. One quarter of these are teenagers.[15] It is estimated that one in four sexually active teens contracts an STD each year.[16]

Condoms and Consistency
Remember the earlier definition of safe sex?

> *"Condoms, if used consistently and correctly, are very effective at preventing pregnancy and the transmission of STDs and HIV."*

For condoms to most effectively reduce the risk of teens contracting some STDs, or becoming pregnant, they must be used consistently and correctly.

How many parents have seen their teens do anything consistently and correctly – make up their beds, clean their rooms, take out the trash, feed and walk the dog, mow the grass? That's why they are called adolescents – inconsistency and incorrectness rule!

Is "consistently and correctly" even possible for adults? Research indicates that on the average, only 21 percent of motivated adults used condoms consistently and correctly.[17] Other studies show only half of the most motivated group of adults (those with a partner who is HIV-infected) used condoms consistently.[18] How effective would you rate condoms as a "safe-sex" protection strategy?

Abstinence-Plus Education Is Not About Abstinence

Abstinence-Plus education says it teaches teens how to be abstinent. They do mention abstinence, but research shows that only 5 percent of the content in these programs is actually about abstinence.[19] They also have a message that goes beyond that – a "but, if you can't wait" message. Their message is mixed, and is heard by many teens as advocacy for sexual behavior. Abstinence-Plus education is about *how to* have sex in one form or another. Teens are told that sexual activities other than intercourse are "not sex" and to make up their own minds about when they feel ready to engage in sexual activities. The primary focus of these curricula is on encouraging young people to use contraception. And, most of these "safe-sex" or abstinence-plus advocates do not encourage teens to involve their parents in their decisions.

The truth is that abstinence-plus programs are not about abstinence.

Here is the abstinence-plus message from the Planned Parenthood Web site for teens called *Teenwire.*

"There are two kinds of abstinence. In the first kind, partners have only very limited sex play – maybe you kiss, but there's no nakedness, no groping, no orgasms, nothing. This is the type encouraged by your parents, probably, and it's the right choice for most kids for a long time. This is what Planned Parenthood calls 'abstinence'.

"The second kind includes lots of sex play and is more open to possibilities, as long as partners don't have vaginal, oral, or anal intercourse. Planned Parenthood calls this type 'outercourse'. Hours of kissing sounds nice, huh? How about a little mutual masturbation that ends with orgasm?" [20]

What Does It Mean to Be Abstinent?

One precocious eighth-grader defined abstinence as "missing school." Teens wonder: Is it a temporary state of sexual inactivity that varies from week to week? Does it only involve penetrative sexual intercourse and not other sexual actions? The definition we at *Choosing the Best* use with students using our curriculum is:

"Abstinence is making an informed decision not to engage in at-risk sexual activities including sexual intercourse, anal sex, oral sex, and mutual masturbation."

Besides the emotional consequences of oral sex, many of the most common STDs, including HIV, can be spread through oral sex with an infected partner. Mutual masturbation, like oral sex, allows for the exchange of bodily fluids and therefore is also an at-risk sexual behavior.

It's Not Sex If

Some teens think they are being abstinent if they don't participate in sexual intercourse. These teens, however, are involved in mutual masturbation, oral sex, rubbing against one another in the genital area without clothes, and heavy petting with or without clothing. Here's a sample of their thinking:

"It's not sex if there's no penetration."

"It's not sex if we keep our clothes on (said about mutual masturbation or petting)."

"It's not sex if the girl doesn't climax."

"Oral sex is not sex, because there are no consequences and no responsibilities."

"Oral sex is not sex, because there are no emotional attachments."

"It's not sex because you can do it (mutual masturbation, oral sex) with anyone, but you save sex (intercourse) for that special one."

By choosing abstinence until marriage, a teen receives **freedom.**

• **freedom to** pursue goals and dreams for their future.

• **freedom from** getting an STD, becoming pregnant, feeling guilty, worrying about what others think, developing poor self-esteem, and other negative outcomes of sex before marriage.

Teens need to hear the abstinence message often and from numerous sources. The message cannot be about postponing sex until a teen is 17 or 18; the risks and consequences of sexual activity are the same at 18. Studies indicate that at least 50 percent of sexually active men and women acquire HPV at some point in their lives.[21] The message cannot be about having sex when you find true love; people at every age think they've found true love. The message cannot be about using other methods of sex play that can still expose your teen to emotional and disease risks. The message must be that the only way to have a healthy future and eliminate sexual risks is to choose abstinence until marriage.

To provide the best future for our teens, we as parents must be consistent about this message. We must communicate that "abstinence only" is the way to go, not "abstinence plus."

Parent: Let's Think About It!

As you have read, one of the most important parts of helping your teen choose abstinence is to decide what you believe. Use the following scale to evaluate your beliefs.

1 I completely disagree.
2 I slightly disagree.
3 I have no opinion one way or the other.
4 I agree most of the time.
5 I totally agree.

_____ 1. I can make a difference in the life of my teenager.

_____ 2. I deliver straightforward, unmixed messages about sex to my teen.

_____ 3. The "safe sex" message is not healthy or acceptable for my teen.

_____ 4. Abstinence involves not only abstaining from sexual intercourse, but also abstaining from sexual "outercourse."

_____ 5. Mutual masturbation or touching the other person's genitals is not healthy or acceptable behavior for teens.

_____ 6. Oral sex is not healthy or acceptable behavior for teens.

_____ 7. Condoms do not eliminate the risk of a teen pregnancy.

_____ 8. Condoms do not eliminate the risk of contracting STDs.

_____ 9. The only message to give teens is: **Abstinence is the best preparation for your future.**

_____10. Not all teen Web sites related to sexual issues have reliable information.

What Do You Think?

1. Were you sexually active as a teenager? Before you got married? Presently, if you are a single parent?

2. How does your past (or present) affect what you say to your teen about the teen's sexual activity?

3. What have you told your teen about what is healthy and acceptable sexual behavior, and what isn't and where to draw the line?

4. What have you told your teen about who is responsible for setting sexual limits in a relationship? What limit do you believe is best for a teen?

Parent and Teen: Let's Talk About It!
Discussion Three – Abstinence and "Safe Sex"

1. **The Debate Continues.** Steve and Tony continue their discussion of sex begun in Step One. This time their conversation takes a different twist. After reading their discussion, check whether you agree or disagree with each guy's statements. Write down some key thoughts as to why you agree or disagree. Discuss your thoughts with your parent.

> **Tony:** *"Sex is not always a sure thing; why take the risk? You could get a disease or get stuck with a kid for the rest of your life."*

> **Steve:** *"You use protection. Say you're in the 11th-grade, you've known this girl for two years, you know everything about her, and you know she doesn't have any diseases, and she wants to do it and you want to do it. Why wouldn't you do it? I would do it in the 8th-grade because you use protection, and you know nothing can go wrong."*

> **Tony:** *"There are so many things that can go wrong. Condoms break and then look at where you are. There are too many things I want to do with my life than to take a chance of messing it up, even before I get out of school."* [1]

How does Tony feel about sex before marriage? _____

_____

Do you . . .
❏ Agree   ❏ Disagree

What does Steve think will protect him if he has sex before marriage?

_____

Do you . . .
❏ Agree   ❏ Disagree

2. **The "Safe-Sex" Message.** Some teens (and adults) believe that a person can have "safe sex." "Safe sex" or "safer sex" means the male uses a latex (rubber) condom to reduce the risk of getting a sexually transmitted disease or of an unwanted pregnancy. Check the messages about "safe sex" that you have heard:

❏ Condoms are 98 percent effective in protecting against STDs and pregnancy when used consistently and correctly.

❏ Although condoms don't provide 100 percent protection against AIDS or other sexually transmitted diseases, they are highly effective.

❏ Girls cannot get pregnant when their partners use condoms.

❏ Condoms protect you from sexually transmitted diseases.

❏ It's best to avoid sex until you get married, but if you can't, use a condom.

3. **Check Out the Facts!** Check out these facts, and fill in the missing words. (It's OK to guess.) Answers are at the end of this section.

 ❖ *Condoms fail*

   ◆ Because latex condoms are made of rubber, they can _____ _____ and _____ _____.

   ◆ Typical couples who use condoms for birth control experience a first year failure rate of _____ in preventing pregnancy.[2] This means that over a period of four years, there could be close to a _____ percent chance of getting pregnant when using condoms for birth control.[3]

 Which of the following would you do if you knew the annual failure rate was 15 percent?

   ❏ A roller coaster ride
   ❏ An airplane flight
   ❏ Skydiving
   ❏ Bungee jumping

❖ *Condoms do not eliminate the risk of contracting STDs*

Here's what the research shows – when used every time, condoms are:

◆ Most effective against HIV, reducing the risk by _____ versus not using a condom at all. However, 15 percent of the risk remains for a life-threatening disease with no cure.[4]

◆ Approximately _____ effective in reducing the risk of STDs spread by body fluid, such as chlamydia, gonorrhea, and trichomoniasis. However, 50 percent of the risk remains.[5]

◆ Less effective in reducing the risk of STDs spread by skin-to-skin contact (eg., herpes, syphilis, etc.). Condoms offer no protection if the infection is located in an area not covered by a condom.[6]

◆ _____ effective in reducing the risk for HPV, the most common viral STD. However, some risk reduction may occur with HPV-related symptoms (e.g. warts and cervical cancer).[7]

◆ What is the only certain way to eliminate the risk of contracting an STD or experiencing an unintended pregnancy? _____

_____

4. **Defining Abstinence.** Let's be sure everyone is working from the same definition. Abstinence is making an informed decision to *not engage* in sexual behaviors that put a person at risk for getting pregnant, contracting an STD (sexually transmitted disease), or dealing with the emotional damage of sex. Abstinence avoids (check all that apply):

❏ anal sex   ❏ vaginal sex   ❏ oral sex
❏ stimulating another in the genital area

By choosing abstinence until marriage, a teen receives **freedom**.

◆ **freedom to** pursue goals and dreams for your future, and
◆ **freedom from** getting an STD, becoming pregnant, feeling guilty, worrying about what others think, developing a poor self-esteem, and other negative outcomes of sex before marriage.

5. What Do You Think?

♦ List several reasons teens choose to be sexually active and engage in at-risk behaviors: _____

_____

♦ List several reasons teens choose to be sexually abstinent until marriage _____

_____

♦ What do you believe is best? Why? _____

_____

6. What Can Be Totally Eliminated by the Use of Condoms?

Circle the item(s) that can be totally eliminated by using a condom.

jealousy	heartbreak	pregnancy	loneliness
loss of goals	distrust of others	meaningless wedding	STDs
depression	loss of self-esteem	disappointed parents	
not finishing	high school	unstable relationships	

Now, cross out the item(s) that can be eliminated by being abstinent until marriage. _____

_____

Answers for the "Condoms fail" section: (first statement) break, slip off; (second statement) 15 percent, 50 percent.

Answer for "Condoms do not eliminate the risk of contracting STDs" section: (first statement) 85 percent; (second statement) 50 percent; (third statement) not.

4

Step Four

Stress the Rewards

Abstinence Allows for a Promising Future

We asked the teens in our *Choosing the Best* survey why they chose abstinence. Their top three answers were positives, not negatives:

- parental expectations
- the accomplishment of personal goals
- the desire to prepare for marriage

Here are some of their specific responses to the question "Why am I choosing abstinence until marriage?"

"To go to college and have a healthy marriage"

"To finish high school, go to college and start a career"

"To have a healthy marriage and be an elementary school teacher"

"College and sports career"

"Education, travel, and joyful marriage"

"A future with my husband and no STDs"

"Happy and fulfilled marriage"

"Go to college of medicine, get married and live a good life"

"Good stable relationship with my husband, good role model and good family"

"College, find a husband and tell my kids I waited"

"Find the right woman for me, get married and have a family"

The Reward of Achieving Personal Goals

A goal is an achievement that is desired in the future and requires a willingness towards which to work. Teens with clearly defined goals, who see sexual abstinence as one step in reaching those goals, are more likely to remain abstinent. Goals regulate actions and motivate positive behavior. Many teens already understand the power of goals. They may give up free time or accept rigorous training in order to make a sports team or cheerleading squad, to earn a part in a drama, to play in the band, or to pass advanced placement classes. They even accept menial jobs to earn money for clothes, computers, or CDs.

The 2002 Winter Olympics gave us numerous examples of young people who sacrificed normal teen activities in order to achieve their goals of winning an Olympic medal. Let's look at two of those contenders.

Apolo Anton Ohno was a teen headed for big trouble with gangs and drugs. His single-parent dad realized he had to do something drastic. Ohno had already traded in his in-line skates for a pair of speed skates and was a national short track champion at 14, but his bad attitude limited his training. So, his father took Ohno to a remote cabin and left him with a week's worth of provisions and the challenge to decide what was important to him. An attitude adjustment and focused training helped Ohno win the gold medal in the 1500-meter short track speed skating event. The night before he had won the silver medal. Both Ohno and his father admit Ohno is a work in progress. Ohno credits his dad for keeping him pointed in the right direction.[1]

Sixteen-year-old Sarah Hughes beat the world's best ice skaters in a huge Olympic upset. Her flawless performance and seven triple jumps won her the gold medal in women's figure skating. Hughes performed what she called "the skate of my life" to win. Soon afterward, she returned to her high school in Hackensack, N.J., to work toward another goal in her life – scoring in the high 1500s on her SATs.[2]

Facing the future is scary, even for adults. Some teens focus on the present more than the future. Younger teens, because of the many changes in their lives, are more self-focused. Young teens may not be thinking about dating, much less marriage. This is normal. Older teens want to know what the future has for them. Goal setting for both groups, however, is possible, and can be a critical motivating factor in their lives.

How To Set Goals

One of the best preventive steps you can take with your teen is to help him or her establish and commit to goals. In the Parent and Teen Discussion section at the end of this chapter, you have an opportunity to work with your teen in goal setting.

The *Choosing the Best* curriculum teaches a three-step process to help your teen learn how to set a goal. The steps are:

• **See It!** Start with a mental picture. What do you see yourself doing in the future? Example: *Is it playing a trumpet or becoming a star athlete?*

• **State It!** Move to a specific statement of intent. Specifically, what do you want to achieve or become? Example: *To play in the school band next fall or make the football team.*

• **Start It!** Begin the process of achieving the goal by taking the first step. What can you do to start working towards your goal? Example: *Start practicing two hours each day.*

Most people think of a goal as a physical achievement. Achievement goals are things a person wants to do in life. Most of us set achievement goals: save for my teen's college education; learn how to program the remote control; stop smoking. For teens, achievement goals range from passing algebra to choosing a college, from deciding what to do on Friday night to deciding what to do after high school.

Your job is to help your teen identify those personal goals. Be sure the teen understands that abstinence plays a key role in achieving those personal goals. You can contrast this with how the consequences of sexual activity will undermine the achievement of those goals.

The Reward of Attaining Personal Freedom

A major reason for the period known as adolescence is to gain freedom. Without achieving freedom, teenagers would remain helpless children, bound by unhealthy family ties. Freedom moves teens into the world where they learn to use self-control and personal boundaries in a positive manner. Freedom is a destination, a goal, and a process.

Initially, teens seek freedom from parents physically by staying out of the house, being with friends, going places on their own. They also hope to achieve emotional freedom by looking for answers in other places, testing family values, not depending on parents for personal acceptance. As they struggle with gaining freedom from parents, they look for freedom to do other things. These usually include learning about themselves, discovering how to get along with others in a healthy manner, experiencing new situations, figuring out how to handle personal decisions, and working towards personal goals.

In Step Three, you saw that personal freedom is one reward for choosing abstinence. By choosing to wait until marriage to have sex, a teen gains:

• **freedom from** worry, guilt, sexually transmitted diseases, unwanted pregnancies, the consequences of pregnancy, and feelings of being used by another.

• **freedom to** take control of life, to like oneself, to work towards personal goals without hindrances, to experience healthy, lasting relationships, and to enjoy being a teenager without financial concerns or emotional baggage.

Many teens don't consider these freedoms until they no longer are available.

The Reward of a Happy Marriage

More than half the goals shared by the teens in our survey relate to preparing for their future marriage. In another unrelated study, 72 percent of the boys and 83 percent of the girls said they look forward to a good marriage and happy family life.[3]

Marriage has much to offer. Researchers know that married people live longer, remain in better health, are more physically active, and have better mental and emotional health than those who are single, cohabitating, or divorced. In addition, married people are less lonely than unmarried people, and are more likely to report they are happy with life.[4]

So what is one of the best ways teens can prepare for a happy marriage? You guessed it – abstinence. Abstinence until marriage contributes positively to a healthy and successful family life.

Guess Who's More Protected Against Divorce?

In their idealistic ways, most teens (55 percent of the guys, 64 percent of the girls) expect to stay married to the same person for life.[5] With so many well-intentioned marriages ending in divorce, how can young people insulate themselves from the tragedy of divorce? You guessed it – abstinence until marriage can help hold the marriage together. A recent study by the CDC found that 20 percent of first marriages end in separation or divorce within five years. In marriages where the couple had lived together, the probability of the marriage ending in five years jumped to 49 percent. After 10 years of marriage, the previously cohabitating couples were twice as likely to get a divorce as those couples who had not been sexually active before marriage.[6] Those who lived with more than one partner before marriage had even higher rates of divorce.

After two years, most cohabitating couples end their relationships by either getting married or separating permanently. After five years, only 10 percent remain together.[7] As the time increases in an uncommitted relationship, the couple's acceptance of marriage and childbearing decreases.[8] Most men postpone a commitment to marriage because by living with a woman they get all the benefits of sex and companionship without any of the responsibilities. As one man put it, "Subconsciously, you know you can always walk out."[9]

Researchers have wondered why married adults who were sexually abstinent until marriage are twice as likely to stay together as married adults who were not abstinent. Perhaps one explanation lies in the beliefs of those who were sexually active outside marriage. If they were less committed to the idea of marriage in the beginning, they may be quicker to leave a marriage. Those who had the self-discipline and the determination to wait until marriage may believe in working through the difficult times.

Guess Who's Producing Happier Children?

Here I'm not talking about your children; I'm talking about your *grandchildren!* Children born into a marriage are in better physical and emotional health, have more stability in life, and have better economic resources. Without marriage, children are left to the whims of adults to stay and provide financial support. Three-quarters of the children born into a situation where the father

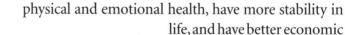

and mother are not married will see their parents leave one another. Only a third of children born to married parents have this experience.[10] That "piece of paper," which represents marriage, ensures that only 9 percent of children in married households live in poverty, compared to 46 percent of children in female-only households.[11]

One reason many of today's marriages fail is that the emphasis is on the wedding, instead of the marriage. Today's teens are not taught how to stay married. They need to know that marriage involves commitment to another person, even when life gets tough. Linda J. Waite and Maggie Gallagher, authors of *The Case for Marriage: Why Married People are Happier, Healthier, and Better Off Financially*, found that even in the worst marriages (other than those involving physical abuse), the couple should stay together. Eighty-six percent who said they were very unhappy in their marriages reported five years later that their attitudes had changed to very happy.[11] Teens need to know that marriages aren't built on sex, but sex can go a long way to making a marriage happier.

Guess Who's Having the Best Sex?

The answer might surprise teens. Faithfully married couples gain more sexual pleasure and emotional satisfaction when compared to all sexually active people.[12] Dr. David Larson, a researcher at the National Institutes of Health, discovered a link between premarital abstinence and sexual satisfaction in marriage. He reports, "Couples not involved before marriage and faithful during marriage are more satisfied with their current sex life than those who were involved before marriage."[13] Other research studies agree that the sex inside of marriage is better.

One research survey of more than 1,000 people discovered that 67 percent of all married adults report that they are "happy with their sex life." Only 45 percent of all singles report the same.[14] Another survey, commissioned by the Family Research Council, (FRC) supports these findings. The FRC report showed that 72 percent of married people said they were "very satisfied" with their sex life. Compare that to the 41 percent of singles who said they had good sex. The satisfied couples also strongly believed that sex outside of marriage is wrong. Of course, these sexually active singles had no objection to sex outside of marriage.[15]

Couples who are sexually involved without being married lack the sense of stability associated with the commitment of marriage. They have higher rates of alcoholism, depression, and domestic violence.[16] Those who do marry after being sexually active experience lower marital satisfaction and substantially higher divorce rates.[17] Authors Waite and Gallagher offer this reason, "One reason married people have more sex is that any single act of sex costs them less in time, money, and psychic energy."[18]

The Value of an Abstinence Pledge

Research shows that teens who make a commitment or pledge to be abstinent until marriage are less likely to become sexually active than those who do not. In fact, researchers were surprised to find that teens who make this pledge delay sexual activity by an average of 18 months.[19]

When Austin was in ninth grade, he signed a pledge to remain abstinent until marriage. In the ninth grade it was easy to sign the pledge because Austin wasn't dating anyone. In the 11th grade Austin started dating Cindy. After a couple of dates, Austin told

Cindy about his abstinence pledge. She had signed a similar pledge. With that information in mind, they planned dates that were fun and active, and they often included others. They avoided places like parties where alcohol was served and everyone paired off, and situations like sitting in a parked car for several hours where they might be tempted.

In the 12th grade, Austin broke off with Cindy and started dating Alicia. Things heated up quickly. That abstinence pledge grew harder to keep, but he was determined. Alicia was determined also, so after only a few months their relationship ended because Austin wouldn't have sex. He often remarked how easy it was to keep his pledge in the ninth grade, when he wasn't dating, and how hard it was to keep his pledge now that he was dating. But Austin found ways to date and not become sexually involved.

In college, the opportunity and availability increased, but Austin stuck with his commitment. He and his main girlfriend Maisie enjoyed numerous activities through both the college and in the city where they attended college. When things grew too passionate in one of their dorm rooms, one would leave, go get a pizza, and return to a less passionate situation. When Austin married, he gave his wife the best possible gift – his purity.

The pledge of abstinence is a starting point for parents and teens. Many parents celebrate their teen's decision by giving the teen a small gift – a commitment ring or a medallion for a necklace. To increase the effectiveness of the pledge, abstinent teens need accountability and regular reinforcement. Encourage your teen to select two or three friends who also are abstinent as accountability partners. One way to reinforce the commitment is to celebrate the anniversary of the teen's commitment by going out to the teen's favorite restaurant. In the Discussion section at the end of this chapter is the Abstinence Pledge. You can discuss the pledge with your teen at this point, or you can wait until you have completed more of the steps to offer your teen the opportunity to sign.

Parent: Let's Think About It!

Once again it's time to check your beliefs, so you can support your teen. Use the following to evaluate your beliefs.

1 I completely disagree.
2 I slightly disagree.
3 I have no opinion one way or the other.
4 I agree most of the time.
5 I totally agree.

_____ 1. Setting goals offers purpose and direction in life.

_____ 2. I have personal goals for my life.

_____ 3. I have family goals that include goals for the future of my teen.

_____ 4. A person can have personal values and still enjoy a wide range of freedom.

_____ 5. It is important that my teen gains emotional, as well as physical, freedom from our family.

_____ 6. Freedom carries with it responsibilities.

_____ 7. I believe in the institution of marriage.

_____ 8. Cohabitation is a threat to a couple's future.

_____ 9. Cohabitation does not have a commitment basis, but a trial basis.

_____10. Within marriage, a couple has the freedom to make sex more fun, more romantic, and more convenient than sexual activity prior to marriage.

Parent and Teen: Let's Talk About It!
Discussion Four – Identify the Rewards

1. **Motivation.** Read these statements from real teens and decide what motivates them to be abstinent.

> *"I am doing a lot of music right now. I play the guitar, and I sing. I'm driven by all these things. I feel like I'm on this road, and I just don't want anybody to mess with me."* [1] (a 15-year-old girl)

> *"I have goals. I have things that I want to do with my life. That's one of the reasons why I'm not having sex. I want to go to college. I want to be somebody."* [2] (a 16-year-old boy)

> *"Sex – it's a big deal, so it's not something I want to worry about right now. My priorities are trying to get into a good college and getting grades and just having a good time."* [3] (a 17-year-old girl)

Your Response _____

_____

2. **Goal Setting.** A **GOAL** is something you **DESIRE** in the future, and are willing to **WORK** towards. There are three steps in goal setting:

◆ **See It**: Start with a mental picture in your mind. What do you see yourself doing in the future? For example: *"I see myself playing the trumpet."*

◆ **State It:** State something specific you want to do, or to become, to move towards your mental picture. For example: *"I want to march in the school band next fall."*

◆ **Start It:** Start by taking the first step towards your goal. For example: *"I will start practicing for an hour each day after school."*

Now, it's your turn to try it:

♦ **See It:** List three things you enjoy doing, like singing, dancing, reading, playing sports, working at the computer etc. _____

_____

Circle one of these you see yourself **doing well** in the future. What can you do with this interest or skill?

♦ **State It:** State one specific thing you will do this year to move towards your future picture. _____

_____

♦ **Start It:** What's the first step you will take to start towards your goal?

_____

Let's think about it! How will choosing to be abstinent until marriage affect your ability to reach this goal, and any other goals, that you want to achieve in your life? _____

_____

3. **More Rewards in Marriage.** Read each goal statement and circle **T** if you think the statement is true or **F** if you think the statement is false. Look up the answers at the end of this section and compare them with your responses.

T	F	1. Most teens have a goal to have a good marriage and a happy family life.
T	F	2. Married people live longer, remain in better health, are more physically active, and have better mental and emotional health than people who are single, cohabitating, or divorced.
T	F	3. Sexually active singles have as good, or better, sex life than married couples.
T	F	4. Married adults who were sexually abstinent until marriage are twice as likely to stay together than those married adults who were not abstinent.
T	F	5. Abstinence before marriage builds more trust into the marriage relationship.

4. **Other Reasons to Choose Abstinence.** Identify why these teens are choosing abstinence until marriage.

> *"I'm actually 20 years old, and I'm still a virgin, and I make that choice because I'm scared of the [diseases]. I come right out and tell them I haven't had sex. I'm still alive and healthy."* [4] (a 20-year-old male)

> *"I'm not ready to have sex. I'm 18, but there are too many diseases out there, and it's like why risk being with somebody just because you feel sexually attracted to them?"* [5] (a 18-year-old girl)

Your Response _____

5. **Abstinence Provides Freedom.** Make a list of what making the decision to be abstinent frees you **from** and what abstinence frees you **to**.

◆ Abstinence provides **freedom from**: _____

_____

◆ Abstinence provides **freedom to**: _____

_____

6. **Making An Abstinence Pledge.** Read the following definition of abstinence.

Abstinence is the
    Best preparation for your future by:

        Choosing not to engage in
at-risk sexual behaviors, including sexual intercourse, oral sex, anal sex, and touching in the genital area.

Making healthy choices is one of the most

CHOOSING ABSTINENCE PLEDGE

Today I choose **Abstinence** as the way to make the **Best** preparation for my future by **Choosing** to wait until marriage to have sex. By making this promise I can be:

◆ free from worry, guilt, sexually transmitted diseases, teenage pregnancy, and feelings of being used by others;
◆ free to control my life, to like myself, to work towards my goals, to have healthy relationships, and to enjoy being a teenager.

Therefore, I promise
my present family
my future family
my friends who support me and
myself to be sexually abstinent until marriage.

Signed: _____ Date: _____

I will ask these people to help me keep this promise:

_____

_____

_____

important decisions you can make as a teen. Read and respond to the following abstinence pledge.

7. How can your parents and others help you keep this pledge?

_____

_____

5

Step Five

Be There

Being Present in Mind and Body

Absentee parents – an old cliché? Not according to these teenagers.

Lathia: "Growing up I wasn't very close with my parents. We didn't talk about personal matters . . . I actually turned to my friends and would talk about sex with my friends, instead of my parents . . . My father has moved on and gotten married, had more kids, that kind of thing. So I guess, it was like me looking for a male figure in my life. You know, looking for that male, dominance to get my life straightened up. [Someone to say] 'This is what I recommend you do' and things like that." [1]

Danna: "My father is very removed from my life. Once I got a little older and realized how removed he was from me, I felt like I didn't really have a father. My mother [was] always very anxious, and I got very angry with her for it. I felt that I was ignored, and that's when I started acting out. In the sixth grade, when I was 11, I started hooking up with guys." [2]

Michelle: "Up until 10 or 12 [years of age], everything was perfect. I mean, my father was there; my mother was there. You know, it was just [that I] didn't see any of the underlying turmoil. Then, when I turned about 10 years old, I remember them fighting a lot. She was gone more and more of the time.

"It was just really bad. So I would try to stay out of the house as much as I could. I started seeing Keith. We were both these damaged kids, and we could relate . . . I just felt like I needed someone . . . to be with me and not leave me."[3]

Not Being There Physically

When one parent isn't present in the lives of the children, the children suffer. Sadly, one of the fastest growing trends in the country involves absentee dads. In 1960, 5.1 million children lived in a home without a father; today that figure has risen to 16.6 million.[4] More than 28 percent of all children currently live apart from their biological fathers. Fatherless homes, unfortunately, have a great impact on both boys and girls.

Absentee Dads Affect Sons and Daughters

• Girls who grow up without a father lose out on the emotional closeness of a male who communicates to his daughter that she is valued and loved.[5]

• Girls from homes where the fathers are not present are more promiscuous, being involved in greater and earlier sexual activity.[6]

• Boys from homes with absentee fathers are more likely to be violent in their behavior and attitudes. They tend to be more aggressive than boys growing up in two-parent households.[7]

• Young males in homes in which there is no fathering influence are twice as likely to become involved in criminal activity. This statistic triples when the fatherless young male lives in a neighborhood with many single-parent families.[8]

Moms and Dads – You Matter!

Conversely, studies have shown that a fathers' presence and involvement promotes his child's well-being. According to the National Fatherhood Initiative, compared to children who have no fathering influence, "children with involved, loving fathers are significantly more likely to do well in school, have healthy self-esteem, exhibit empathy and pro-social behavior, and avoid high-risk behaviors such as drug use, truancy, and criminal activity."[9]

Research also confirms the fact that girls, in particular, benefit greatly from the presence and involvement of their mothers in their lives. For girls, having a close relationship with their mothers has a positive impact on their sexual decision making. One study found, for example, that teenage girls who are close to their mothers are more likely to stay virgins than girls who are not. The mothers whose daughters were virgins also shared the following qualities:

• They strongly disapproved of their daughters having sex.
• They were satisfied with their relationships with their daughters.
• They frequently talked with the parents of their daughter's friends.[10]

Single Parents? What Can You Do?

The statistics point out the key role that both dads and moms play in the healthy relational and sexual development of girls and boys. So, if you're a single parent, what can you do? The first step is to realize that you are vitally important to your family. Your purpose is to guide your teenager from childhood into adulthood – that is a noble, worthwhile calling. The key ingredient is to keep the atmosphere in your home as healthy and loving as possible. As a single parent, your challenge will be greater than in two-parent households.

Let's look at four ways that you, as a single parent, can help your son or daughter during the critical teen years. While these suggestions may seem obvious, perhaps they will spark an idea that you haven't considered.

1. **Show respect for the other parent.** Even if you and your ex-partner don't have a good relationship, try to remain open to letting your teenager share a positive relationship with him or her. Diane Chambers, author of *Solo Parents: Raising Strong and Happy Families* cautions, "Bottom line, divorced parents who see their children as psychological extensions of themselves end up blocking, many times unintentionally, the very healing tonic their kids need – to feel accepted

and loved by both parents."[11] If possible, discuss with your ex-partner the importance of a unified front during the teen years. Try to set up rules and boundaries that work in both households. You may also want to involve your ex-partner in working through *Parents, Teens and SEX: The BIG TALK Book.*

In some cases, however, the other parent may be deceased, unavailable, or unwilling to participate. Because you cannot control the other person, encourage your teenager to talk about this lost relationship. If possible, refrain from making remarks that turn the teenager against the other parent.

2. **Look for role models who can be involved in your teen's life.** These may be youth group leaders, coaches, community club leaders, relatives, even personal friends. Big Brothers Big Sisters of America (www. BBBSA.org) can put you in touch with a local chapter in your area. This outstanding organization matches willing young adults with same-sex children to build positive mentoring relationships.

3. **Join a local support group for single parents of teens.** Your phone directory should have a listing of local chapters. Find a place where you can interact with others on a regular basis, so you can meet other single parents who will be able to offer support and ideas. If a group is not available, spend time with a friend who also has teens and do something fun on a regular basis with your teens.

4. **Be careful not to use your teen as a surrogate spouse or substitute parent.** An older teenage son cannot be a healthy father substitute for younger siblings. He may feel responsible, and in many ways can be a good role model, but he should not be expected to discipline or make decisions about the other children. Similarly, a teenage daughter should not be expected to take care of the household, tend to younger siblings, or take on the responsibilities of a mother who may be absent.

Home, But Not Present

Not all children with problems, however, come from single-parent homes. Many intact homes, where both parents are present, find sons and daughters involved in at-risk behavior. These families don't always come from disadvantaged neighborhoods or live in poverty. When parents are not involved in a healthy way in the lives of their children, the children suffer, no matter what the social or economic situation.

Several years ago, a PBS *Frontline* documentary called "The Lost Children of Rockdale County" recorded the startling sexual behavior of an affluent, upper middle class suburb outside of Atlanta, Georgia. The Rockdale County health department became alarmed by numerous reported cases of syphilis in a group of young teenage girls. In their investigation the county's health team discovered that more than 200 young people were engaged in group sex.

"There was group sex going on in terms of one guy having sex with one of the girls, and then the next guy having sex with the same girl. There was group sex going on in terms of one girl having sex with multiple male partners at the same time, [and] multiple females having sex with each other," according to Professor Claire Sterk, Emory University's School of Public Health.[12] Not only were the teens having sex with multiple partners, "they were having every kind of sexual act that you can do," adds Cynthia Noel of the Rockdale County Public Health Department.[13]

In addition, the teens had access to pornography in different homes and made a game out of doing the things they saw with both the girls and guys. Because of the lack of parental involvement with these 200 teens, viewers and critics renamed the situation, "The Lost Parents of Rockdale County." Let's look at two families who were interviewed for this documentary to better understand the challenge and importance of being emotionally present for our children during the teen years.

"What Happened to My Little Girl?"

Amy was from a close family that spent a lot of time together when she was younger. They went on regular family vacations. Amy's father Frank coached her in softball from the time she was 7 years old until she was 18. Amy was a typical good kid, who lived in an upscale neighborhood with two parents committed to her well-being.

Amy's life changed when she reached her teen years. She had a difficult time adjusting in seventh grade. Her best friend from elementary school rejected her for a new set of friends in middle school, so Amy didn't make many friends after that. In ninth grade, Amy made the cheerleading squad, and things looked up. After being cut from the squad in 10th grade, though, Amy sought acceptance from a different group of friends – teens involved in sex and alcohol. Amy shares what her life was like:

"After that, I felt depressed a lot. I was just real unhappy. I didn't have any kind of friends at school. And I guess I kind of picked the wrong friends outside of school, too . . . A lot times I would be high when I came home, so I really tried not to talk to [my parents] or look at them or anything. I would try just to go down to my room." [14]

Where were Amy's parents during this time? They were home – but not present. Amy's father Frank looks at it this way:

"I knew it was possible that it was happening, that she was sexually active. But we didn't sit down and talk about [it]. I guess we could have talked about what she was doing then, and we didn't . . . We've got TVs in every room in the house. I watch my programs. My wife watches her programs in another room. The kids watch it [in other rooms]. Yeah, we would spend time together, but much of the time spent in the house together was not together." [15]

Frank and his wife completely missed Amy's silent screams for attention and help. Like too many parents who fall into the trap of not being there for their teens during difficult transition times of their lives, they weren't paying close attention.

What do you think happened to Amy? Here's how she describes her experiences.

"[My new group of friends] would buy me alcohol, and so I was happy for a little while. I was always a different person when I was drunk . . . One time, I was at my house and one of my friends was there with me. We got really drunk and [invited] four guys to come over. We let them do whatever they wanted to with us. Later, I just felt really sad and angry with myself, because I knew I couldn't change anything about it. But I just wished it would never happen after it always did." [16]

Amy continued to cry out for help, not by asking, but by her extreme at-risk behavior. How did Frank react?

"I've gone through a lot of tears, but what can you do about it? You know you can't lock a kid in a closet that's 13-, 14-, 15-years old . . . You've just got to hope you've instilled the kind of values in them, what is important, and when they get old, they will respect [those values]. I feel helpless . . . I don't believe I could put enough pressure on my family and my daughter to overcome the kind of social pressure they have out there." [17]

At this point you're probably screaming, "Why don't you just talk to her? Why can't you be there for her?" Frank struggled with parenting his teenage daughter. He didn't know how to be available for Amy. (Amy's mother refused to be interviewed for the documentary). While this real-life story didn't turn out with a happy ending, let me share another story from the same documentary that happened between a single-parent mom and her daughter.

"I'll Do Whatever it Takes!"

Heather's mother Pat and her father divorced when Heather and her older brother were small. In order to support the family, Pat began building a career of her own. At the same time, Pat worked on a graduate degree that finally paid off financially. Her full-time corporate job often took her out of town leaving Heather at home alone. On the surface, things were going well. Pat explained why she made the choices she did:

"We are financially better off than we were. Heather has the Tommys and the Filas and whatever name clothes that the kids [wear] out there. At least it makes her feel she's as good as everybody else." [18]

Heather viewed her mother's life this way:

"I like it better when she's gone than when she's at home. I like it better alone than I do with parents." [19]

Do teens get along better without parents? Would most teens agree with Heather? Or, was her toughness another way she was crying out for help? Heather took advantage of her mother's absence one night when she was 12. She snuck out of her house and got drunk. This is what Heather remembers:

"The next thing I know, I wake up and I'm in a room, and I don't have my pants on and so, I mean, I really couldn't call it rape because, you know, I put myself in that position in the first place."

After the incident, to bury the pain, Heather drank more while also turning to drugs. Pat failed to notice her daughter's behavior. When she and Heather were at home, they didn't spend much time together. In fact, they didn't even eat dinner together. Pat reflects:

"She goes up to her room and either takes her school books and studies or watches whatever TV channel she can pick up for the evening. I usually go in [my bedroom]. I like listening to radio. So I would put on the radio, or I have my laptop from work. I'll go to my bedroom and do work there and have my dinner there." [20]

Finally, Heather couldn't take her life anymore. She told her mom about barely being sober for three or four years. She explained about doing drugs almost every day, and she also told her about the rape and the sexual promiscuity. Pat immediately quit her job and started working out of her home. That allowed her not only to spend more time at home with Heather, but also to BE THERE for Heather. In their own words, here's how they explain the ending of their story:

Pat: *"Once I took control, she has done so much better. I mean, it's just night and day. I think she was crying out for help, and I was too busy to hear."*

Heather: "I've taken my second vow. I'm a [renewed] virgin. I have been since the beginning of the 10th grade. I started thinking about what I was going to be when I get older and how I was supposed to get there and what my reputation is like and what I needed to do to change that. So, I've changed a lot of things around." [21]

The producers of "The Lost Children of Rockdale County" quickly point out that Rockdale County represents communities across America. Stories similar to those of Rockdale County occur in many different homes; there are many parents in a variety of neighborhoods who are oblivious, unconcerned or misdirected about how to raise their children. They fail to parent in ways that give their children guidance and clear boundaries. These two real-life stories from the PBS *Frontline* program show the essentials needed for parents to have a good relationship with teens and to be there for them; they also show the consequences of parents not being there for their teens. Let's look at five fatal excuses parents can give for not being there.

Five Fatal Excuses

Excuse #1: "I'm too busy earning a living . . . so I can give my family what they want." Some parents work 40, 60, even 80 hours a week. Unfortunately, parents fail to realize that they only have their teens for a few more years.

Excuse #2: "We each have our own interests. We may be at home, but we're not doing things together." Time in the same house doesn't equal quality time face to face with your teen.

Excuse #3: "She just doesn't listen to me anymore." It's normal for teens to move away from their families physically, emotionally, and socially. At the same time, it is important to remember that you are still the parent. Teens are not adults, and remain in need of guidance and patience. This is not the time to step back and hope you've taught them right from wrong.

Excuse #4: "This cannot happen to my teenager!" Parents believe there are two kinds of kids – theirs and all the others. Sometimes it is easier to be in denial about what is really going on in the life of your child than to face the hard, cold facts. But, denying the problem doesn't help you or your teen.

Excuse #5: "It's not my fault. I did the best I could as a parent."
For some, it's easier to blame others than to see flaws in ourselves – or to fault external factors such as TV, society, schools. Are you willing to sacrifice your teen's future for your shortcomings?

Tips From Our Teen Experts

Let's find out what our team of teen experts say about their relationships with their parents. Nine out of ten teens rated their relationship with their parents as "good to excellent." Check out how these teens described their relationships with their parents:

"Awesome - great communication!"
"It's excellent. I love them with all my heart."
"It's a great relationship, they trust me and love each other."
"Great! We have fun together, we always do cool things, like shopping."
"Wonderful - best parent-kid relationship I know of."
"Wonderful. They are always there for me and support me, but allow me enough room to be my own person."
"We get along well. We fight sometimes, but always work through our issues."

How do positive, healthy parental relationships encourage a teen's decision to be abstinent? According to these teens, the positive relationship between parent and teen is a vital ingredient for inspiring sexual abstinence until marriage. Other studies support this idea. When teens feel highly connected to their parents and experience warm, caring, supportive behavior, they are less likely to become sexually active.[22] Let's see how this happens.

Build a Positive, Healthy Relationship with Your Teen

One of the most important things you can do as a parent is to build and maintain a positive relationship with your teenager during these turbulent teen years. Teens feel strong relationship bonds when they see that their parents not only love them, but also like them. And, if you like them, you want to spend time together, to talk, and to share in their lives. Sadly, some parents view teens as projects to complete, instead of young people worth getting to know.

Our teen experts were asked how to build a stronger relationship between parents and teens. Let's look at five tips they offered.

Tip 1: Be There for a Daily "Touch Time"

Teens spell love as T•I•M•E. After all, it's hard to have a decent relationship with someone you rarely see. Remember when you put you child to bed and read a bedtime story? Remember when you tossed the ball every day? Or, how about the times you and your child sat on the steps and wondered what a butterfly did at night or how a squirrel could jump from limb to limb without falling? Well, even though they're a little taller and busier now, you can take a few minutes each day for a daily touch time.

Five Tips for Being There for Your Teen

Tip 1: Be there for a daily touch time.
Tip 2: Be there on a weekly basis.
Tip 3: Be there by doing fun things together.
Tip 4: Be there with open communication.
Tip 5: Be there for their special events.

Dan tells how he tries every night to stop by his teen's room for some conversation and daily "touch time." While they talk, they often share about their daily struggles, disappointments, and triumphs.

Another parent runs with her teens. Although they don't talk while they run, they build bridges by just doing something together. Another family walks the family dogs together (it takes several to walk the large dogs), and although they aren't talking face to face, they do talk.

Some teens grow more talkative in direct proportion to the lateness of the hour. For some unknown reason, our son Brannon wanted to talk at bedtime. Since he and my wife Donna were the family night owls, he had someone to talk to.

Finding some time each day to stay in touch with your teen can reap huge rewards.

Tip 2: Be There for a Special Weekly Time
In addition to some time daily, set aside a longer time on weekends to stay in touch. This longer time gives opportunities for parents and teens to interact. Call it game night, or video evaluation night, or eating with the family, or whatever you can do together. Here's how it worked for us.

Once our son Brannon started to drive, it became harder to count on having a family time together. So, we had a family meeting and decided that Sunday night would be our special family meal and talk-time together. While we made exceptions, everyone knew Sunday night was a family time. Sometimes we had really important matters to discuss, such as family vacations, scheduling events, or expressing concerns. At other times we used the time for light  conversation, with family members sharing an activity, event, or highlight from their lives during the previous week.

Bobby takes his teens out to eat breakfast once a week at a fast-food place on their way to school. Once his oldest child started driving everyone still drove to the fast-food place, then the son drove the younger teens to school, as dad headed for work.

When Brannon was a teenager, I found the best way to stay in touch with him – to learn about his friends, his interests, and his struggles – was to take him out to eat once a week. An amazing phenomenon occurred! When the food arrived at the table, his mouth opened, not only to eat, but also to talk. At home quite often I got disinterested grunts, rolled eyes, and brief, one-syllable comments.

Tip 3: Be There by Doing Fun Things Together

Some parents become "professional parents." They follow what the latest parenting book says, always being the person in authority, and dispensing all the right answers. Teens find it hard to relate to this professional approach. Sometimes you just need to enjoy your kids again.

When our children where young, we played family football together – my wife Donna and son Brannon against daughter Natalie and me. We have great memories of rolling together on the ground trying to recover a loose football. As the children got older, we moved to playing tennis as a family.

During the teen years, family cookouts offered some entertaining times, as different family members prepared the evening meal. And, of course, family vacations were another time to build family memories. Even small events such as a Saturday hike or a trip to the ballpark added to the family bank account of fun.

Of course, as parents, we must be willing to laugh at ourselves. Develop family jokes or key words that create laughter in which all family members can participate.

Tip 4: Be There with Open Communication

This tip can be difficult if your teen pulls away and refuses to talk. Or, perhaps you are a parent who feels uncomfortable with confrontation, so you handle problems in silence. Although it may be uncomfortable for you or your teen, it really is important to talk.

First, be sure there is real communication. Stephanie went to a party at a friend's house after a ball game. When she saw the other teenagers pull out alcohol and drugs, she left and drove home. When her mom asked why she was home early, Stephanie told her. Instead of applauding her teenager for being smart enough to know when to leave, her mother blew up, blaming Stephanie for going to a party without asking permission. "You know you're not supposed to go to parties without asking," her mother chastised. Stephanie replied, "Actually, mom, you've never told me how you felt about parties. I had to figure it out for myself." Later, her mother admitted that she had never talked to Stephanie about any social behavior.

In their book *How to Talk So Kids Will Listen & Listen So Kids Will Talk*, Adele Faber and Elaine Mazlish developed the idea of making sure the child knows you are listening. Some call this skill "active listening." Others don't know it has a name; they just know that teens respond to it. Here's how it works.

Your daughter wants to go to a spend-the-night-party at the house of a friend whose parents are out of town. Your daughter opens with, "Everyone else is going" and closes with "You never let me go anywhere." Before rendering a decision, restate what you've heard your daughter say, "You want to go to the party because everyone else is going, and you will feel left out and unaccepted if you don't go. And you also feel trapped because we are selective about the places you go. Is that how you feel?"

After you make sure you've heard your teenager's feelings, you can state yours. You may choose to say "No" after all is said: "I am not comfortable with you doing that. Let's come up with another alternative." In other words, you may say "No" in an emphatic way. This is called active listening.

Active Listening

• Acknowledges that the teenager has feelings. By identifying those feelings and restating them, you empathize with your teenager. By recognizing her feelings, you validate her as a person. You express that she has feelings and ideas that are worth hearing.

• Encourages you to remember the intense social pressures of the teen years.

• Allows you to share your feelings, too. ("Here's how I feel about this situation.") Keep this part short and focused.

• Invites your teenager to offer a solution. Be willing to listen. Don't pass judgment on the idea too quickly.

• Helps you make a well-thought-out decision. Give yourself permission to think about it for an hour or a day before giving your teenager an answer.

Communication can also be non-verbal:

• Write your teen a supportive note before a big test and slip it under her door or tuck it in his book bag.

• Send an e-mail of encouragement.

• Leave a post-a-note on the mirror to say you love the teen.

• Place a small gift (new CD, fast-food coupons, movie passes) on a teen's pillow as a thank you for a fun time together.

Tip 5: Be There for Their Special Events

Parents can become so wrapped up in our own situations – jobs, relationships, and pressures – that we can forget the lives of our teens.

We end up sacrificing our children's future for our present concerns.

When my children were younger, I coached each child's soccer team. I figured this would keep me involved in their lives and help me know their friends. This idea worked well in the early years. In the teen years, however, the last thing a teen wants is to have dad hanging around while the teen tries to develop personal freedom. However, being visible for special events communicates a lot of love to a teen.

Special events should include those things that are important to your teen – sporting events, school assemblies, parent-teen activities, performances. Just showing up sends the strong message to the teen that "You are important to me, and I care about you."

Is Your Family An Exception?

"Easy for you to say. You're not a single parent trying to raise kids and hold down a couple of jobs with no other adult support."

"How can I do this? The divorce agreement doesn't let me see my teenager except every other weekend, and sometimes even that's difficult with her busy schedule."

"My teen is almost a legal adult. I'm kidding myself if I think I can make a difference now."

"OK. I already have enough of a guilt trip for not being 'The World's Greatest Parent'. I can't do all this."

It is never too late to put these tips into practice. And you cannot do too little, unless you don't try at all. It wouldn't be the real world if all parents could avoid the excuses and carry out those five tips all the time. Let me encourage you, however, to think of creative ways to incorporate these ideas into time with your teen.

• If you only see your teen every other week, plan a fun activity one weekend a month, letting the teen choose.

• Traveling parents can still call, e-mail, and send cards of encouragement.

• Going to all their games may be impractical, but watching that special game or that one performance or whatever important activity your teen does helps your teen feel significant.

• Start with one idea, and try to find a way to incorporate it into your family's life. After a couple of months, try another one. If something doesn't work the first time, don't give up; try again.

Parent: Let's Think About It!

Take this brief test to analyze how much you are really there for your teen. Tally your answers to assess how you are doing at being there.

1. Each day I spend (a) 15 minutes (b) 30 minutes (c) an hour (d) less than 15 minutes (e) more than one hour talking with my teen. (Do not count the time you spend giving instructions or lecturing.)
2. Each week I spend (a) 30 (b) 40 (c) 50 (d) 60 hours away from my family.
3. We have (a) one (b) two (c) three (d) four (e) more TVs in our home. Our teenager has a TV in his or her room. (f) yes (g) no.
4. As a family we do something together (a) once a week (b) once a month (c) once every six months (d) once a year. The last activity we did as a family was _____.
5. This family activity usually lasts (a) less than one hour (b) more than one hour, but less than two hours (c) more than two hours, but less than three hours (d) an evening (e) a full day.
6. The last vacation we took as a family was (a) this year (b) one year ago (c) two years ago (d) more than two years ago.

Based on your answers, tally your points:

1. (a) 5; (b) 10; (c) 20; (d) 0; (e) 25   My points _____
2. (a) 20; (b) 15; (c) 5; (d) 0   My points _____
3. (a) 1; (b) 2; (c) 3; (d) 4; (e) 3; (f) 0; (g) 10   My points _____
4. (a) 20; (b) 15; (c) 10; (d) 5   My points _____
5. (a) 5; (b) 10; (c) 15; (d) 20   My points _____
6. (a) 20; (b) 10; (c) 5; (d) 0   My points _____

> • If you have 100 to 120 points, this is the ideal, but are you being honest with yourself? Most of us may hope for this, but find it hard to accomplish.
> • If you have 75 to 95 points, you are making a great effort. Keep up the good work. Look for places to improve.
> • If you have 55 to 70 points, you are maintaining, just hanging on. You urgently need to find time to spend with your teen.
> • If you have 30 to 50 points, you have slipped into the danger zone. Your lack of connection leaves your teen open to the friendships of others who may not have your teen's best interests in mind.
> • If you have 10 to 25 points, you need to wear a name tag when you are home. Your teens no longer know who you are.

Parent and Teen: Let's Talk About It!
Discussion Five – Being There

1. **Heather and Pat.** Heather's father and mother divorced when Heather and her older brother were younger. Pat threw herself into building a career and frequently traveled out of town. From Pat's standpoint, her hard work was paying off. Read the following real-life interviews with Pat and Heather.

> **Pat:** "*We were financially better off than we ever were. Heather had the name-brand clothes that all the kids have out there. At least it made her feel she's as good as everybody else. I gave Heather a lot of freedom. She would go to her room and either take her schoolbooks and study or watch TV. I'd usually go to my room for the evening. I prefer listening to the radio. So, I would turn on the radio, and have my laptop with some work. I'd have my dinner in my room, and Heather would eat her dinner in her room.*" [1]

However, Heather's life was going downhill fast.

> **Heather:** "*When I was 12, and my mom was out of town, I went to a party and got pretty drunk. The next think I know, I wake up and I'm in a room without my clothes on. I really couldn't call it rape, because, you know, I put myself in that position in the first place. I didn't tell anybody. Over the next two years I started drinking more, doing some drugs, and having sex with a number of guys. My mom didn't seem to notice what was going on.*" [2]

◆ What effect do you think Pat's absence had on Heather?
◆ Why didn't Pat and Heather spend time together and talk when Pat was home?
◆ Why is it important for parents to be involved in their teen's life?
◆ What advice would you give to Pat and Heather?

2. **The "New" Heather and Pat.** Here's what happened to Heather and Pat. Eventually, Heather couldn't bear her pain alone anymore. She told her mom not only about doing drugs almost every day and about

being drunk all the time, but also about her rape and sexual activity. Pat immediately quit her job, started another job where she could work out of her home, and stayed involved in Heather's life. Read what happened and discuss the questions.

> **Pat:** *"Once I took control, Heather has done so much better. I mean it's just like night and day. I think she was crying out for help, and I was too busy to hear."*

> **Heather:** *"I've taken my second vow. I'm a "renewed" virgin. I have been since the beginning of the 10th-grade. I started thinking about what I was going to be when I get older and how I was supposed to get there and what my reputation is like and what I needed to do to change that. So, I've changed a lot of things around with my mom's help."* [3]

◆ Why did Pat quit her job?

◆ What was the effect on Heather's life?

◆ What is "renewed virginity" and why do you think more and more teens who have been sexually active are choosing "renewed virginity"?

3. **Five Tips for Parents "Being There."** Listed below are five tips for parents to "be there" for their teen. Discuss and evaluate the questions on a scale of 1 to 5 (with 1 being the lowest and 5 being the highest).

❖ **A Daily "Touch Time"** – Some time each day when parent and teen touch base.

	Parent	Teen
◆ How important is this to us?	1 2 3 4 5	1 2 3 4 5
◆ How well are we doing?	1 2 3 4 5	1 2 3 4 5
◆ How can we improve this?	_____	

✎ ❖ **A Special "Weekly Time"** – A longer time once a week to connect and interact.

                                               Parent   Teen
- ◆ How important is this to us? 1 2 3 4 5   1 2 3 4 5
- ◆ How well are we doing?   1 2 3 4 5   1 2 3 4 5
- ◆ How can we improve this? _____

❖ **Doing Fun Things Together** – Doing fun activities together.

                                               Parent   Teen
- ◆ How important is this to us? 1 2 3 4 5   1 2 3 4 5
- ◆ How well are we doing?   1 2 3 4 5   1 2 3 4 5
- ◆ How can we improve this? _____

❖ **Open Communication** – Sharing with each other what's really going on.
- ◆ How important is this to us?

     Parent   Teen
    1 2 3 4 5   1 2 3 4 5
- ◆ How well are we doing?

     Parent   Teen
    1 2 3 4 5   1 2 3 4 5

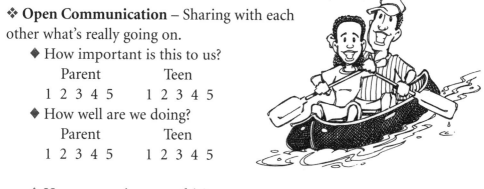

- ◆ How can we improve this? _____

❖ **Being There For Special Events** – Parents being present at important teen events and activities.

                                               Parent   Teen
- ◆ How important is this to us? 1 2 3 4 5   1 2 3 4 5
- ◆ How well are we doing?   1 2 3 4 5   1 2 3 4 5
- ◆ How can we improve this? _____

4. **Parent/Teen Relationship Inventory.** Respond to these statements below as they relate to your relationship. Teen, write **T** next to your response. Parent, write **P** next to your response. When you both have marked your choices, discuss the similarities and differences in your responses.

◆ Identify the words that best describe your family:

respectful	destructive	divided	confused
strained	fun-loving	disruptive	united
focused	encouraging	too busy	forgiving
dysfunctional	not caring	energized	enjoyable

◆ The one word or phrase that best describes our relationship is:
Awesome   Very Good   OK   Not So Good   Distant
Volatile

◆ The one word or phrase that best describes our time together:
Awesome   Very Good   OK   Not So Good   Distant
Volatile

◆ The one word or phrase that best describes our communication is:
Awesome   Very Good   OK   Not So Good   Distant
Volatile

◆ **Teen:** What do you like best about your family? _____
_____

◆ **Parent:** What do you like best about your family? _____
_____

◆ **Teen:** What is your main suggestion for improving the relationship climate in your home? _____
_____

◆ **Parent:** What is your main suggestion for improving the relationship climate in your home? _____
_____

6

Step Six

Build Self-Esteem
Communicating
"You Are Special and Significant"

Self-esteem is tested, examined, altered, inflated, and deflated as a child grows through the teen years. Throughout middle school and high school, feelings of doubt and discouragement bombard the budding genius who did so well in elementary school. Many changes in an emerging teen can aggravate feelings of self-doubt. Volatile emotions and raging hormones add to the stress of a developing self-esteem. Unfortunately, teens with low self-esteem can make life-changing mistakes. Here are some teens' stories, three of whom you heard from in Step Five.

Lathia: In Step Five, Lathia shared the story of her family – or lack of one. Lathia began having sex with older guys when she was 14. She thought older guys would give her the feelings of security she was missing from her family. She soon realized that each guy used her just to get sex. Lathia states:

> *"Being used lowers your self-esteem. It makes you feel like less [of] a woman. You think that you're an object of some sort. Going into other new relationships, you put yourself in worse relationships, like abusive relationships."*[1]

Eldon: Eldon's parents didn't talk to him about sex. What he learned, he discovered on his own. Eldon began having sex because he wasn't getting love and support from his family. He wanted to be loved by somebody. Each time he got into a relationship, he got hurt. Here's how Eldon explained his feelings:

> *"Well, [I thought] if I have sex with this person, that would totally change the relationship, change the outlook, change how she looked at me. She would have to love me. She would have to be with me. When I did have sex with her, I guess really it didn't change anything. I felt like, 'Well, dang, I had sex with her.' I felt bonded with her, and she didn't feel the same way."* [2]

Danna: When Danna was in middle school, several guys offered her and a friend a ride home. Her girlfriend escaped, but Danna was sexually assaulted for more than two hours. After that incident, she tried to take control of her life by deciding when to have sex. Her painful cry comes through in her words:

> *"I was sleeping with so many people. Of course, I was trying to feel better about myself. I really didn't like myself. I didn't like the way people viewed me. I really felt the need to be cared for. I've begged boys to hold me. It was very brief, that feeling of security, for those ten minutes or that hour."* [3]

These painful examples support what researchers report – that there is a significant relationship between self-concept and how a teen behaves. In fact, a recent study found that girls with high self-esteem were three times more likely to remain virgins than those who do not have high self-esteem.[4] Poor self-esteem is a characteristic of teens involved in at-risk behaviors. Among the consequences resulting from low self-esteem are poor academic achievement, crime, violence, teenage pregnancy, drug and alcohol abuse, school dropouts, dating violence, smoking, eating disorders, and suicide.

Our *Choosing the Best* group survey of 100 abstinent teens confirms the important role of self-esteem in encouraging abstinence in a teen's life. More than 90 percent of those surveyed indicated feelings about themselves that showed a strong sense of self-worth.

Parents of teens face a daunting challenge. On one hand, we want to support and encourage our teens to discover who they are and what their life purposes involve. On the other hand, we can't overprotect or control our teens. So what do we do? It all begins with understanding what self-esteem is and how to build it.

Defining Self-Esteem

To help our teenagers through these difficult adolescent years when self-esteem is tested, we must first understand what self-esteem is. The National Association for Self-Esteem defines self-esteem as

> *"The experience of being capable of meeting life's challenges and being worthy of happiness."* [5]

Self-esteem goes beyond feeling good about yourself or learning positive self-talk techniques to recite when doubt occurs. Strong self-esteem is connected to feelings of being worthy, of being loved, and of being competent. Worthiness is the psychological side of self-esteem. Here a person's overall judgment of himself is vital. Competence is the behavioral side of self-esteem. It means that the person feels capable of achieving the desired goal and of making the right choices.

Don't confuse healthy self-esteem with false bravado. Unhealthy self-esteem is seen in teens who are egotistical, conceited, braggarts, bullies, and those who take advantage of others.

Teens with low self-esteem often:

- *are defensive*
- *try to impress others*
- *lack confidence in their abilities*
- *doubt whether they are acceptable to others*
- *are afraid to take risks for fear of failing*
- *blame others for their mistakes*

One study of 1,100 people from ages 7 to 22 found that one characteristic of males who became sexually active as teens was their tendency to rate themselves as better-looking than their peers.[6] Unhealthy self-esteem is acted out in exaggerated behavior.

Remember the Spur Posse? Nine teenage boys from a middle-class community in Lakewood, California were arrested and charged with raping and molesting girls, one of whom was as young as 10 years old. The boys amassed points based on their sexual conquests, seeing each girl as an object, not a person. In court, one father defended his son's actions by saying, "Nothing my boy did was anything that any red-blooded American boy wouldn't do at his age!"[7] Part of the legal defense for the boys was that the culture had caused them to act this way. But the debate outside the courtroom went to a deeper level. It centered on the question of whether teens today are being raised to be cruel or kind.

How to Build Self-Esteem

The role parents play in helping their teens develop positive, healthy self-esteem begins with their own self-esteem. Parents model a positive or negative self-esteem by their personal actions and attitudes. In addition to modeling positive, healthy behavior, parents can influence their teens by providing emotional and physical support.
Through their attitudes and actions, parents let their teens know that the teens are worthy, that they are loved, and that they are capable.

The triangle is one of the strongest structural designs. In fact, engineers use triangles because they can withstand significant pressure and force against them. The strongest type of triangle is one in which all sides are equal.

A triangle with equal sides visually represents the self-esteem building process. Each side of the triangle represents an action and attitude related to the three elements that build self-esteem in a teen. One side is affirmation, which produces feelings of being worthy. Another side is affection, which generates feelings of being loved. The third side is achievement, which results in feelings of competence.

affection

affirmation

achievement

In the same way, a parent's approach to building self-esteem should be balanced, including the three elements of affirmation, affection, and opportunities for achievement.

Unfortunately, achievement sometimes becomes the main focus; affection and affirmation become secondary or may be dependent upon achievement. This imbalance may happen when the parent is applying pressure to the teen to excel in certain 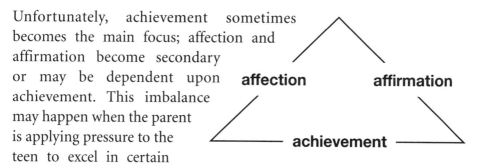 sports or in certain subjects, to be socially active in specific clubs and organizations – all of which may look good on a college application. This often happens when a parent lives out his own dream through the child's achievements. The teen gets the message that achievements build self-worth. This type of imbalance may result in the false self-esteem of egotism or arrogance. Or, if the parent expects perfection, or the teen perceives that the parent expects perfection, the teen may choose dangerous behaviors. Drugs and alcohol can drown out the fear of failure. Eating disorders in teens can become one way to control life. Sexual promiscuity may occur when a teen looks for the missing ingredients of love and acceptance in unacceptable places.

Without achievement, however, the self-esteem triangle gets squeezed with heavy emotions and no strong foundation. This imbalance makes it susceptible to being toppled easily by criticism.

Praise and affirmation can be tricky. Well-intentioned praise rings hollow if the teen knows there is no real "self-achievement" to back it up. Teenagers hone in on fake, unsubstantiated praise. Here are a few examples of how praise can backfire:

"You're such a good student. I'm so proud of you." This can create self-doubt and end up focusing on a weakness, if the teen is struggling in school.

"You'll really stand out in a crowd." This may cause denial and even make the teen feel threatened, especially if the teen's goal is to blend in.

"You played a terrific game." Praise not backed up by reality can be manipulative, leaving the teen to wonder, "What does he want now?"

So, how does a parent balance the building of all three elements of self-esteem during the critical teen years? Let's turn to our *Choosing the Best* survey experts. Here's what they shared about what their parents did to impact their lives.

The Affirmation Angle
In the *Choosing the Best* survey, 98 percent of abstinent teens felt affirmed. Read a sampling of their comments about how their parent(s) affirmed them:

"Tell me they love me everyday and always ask me questions about my day and my life."

"Tell me frequently they are proud of me, compliment me on my goals and just being me."

"Praise me when I do something good and reassure me they still love me when I fail at something."

"Support my extracurricular activities, always coming to my soccer games."

"Tell me how much they love me, ask about my day and do special things for me out of the blue."

"Talk to me like they talk to their friends."

"Write notes about how much they love me, say I love you every day, spend time talking with me."

The last comment was from an 18-year-old, which makes it easy to see that teens never outgrow the need to be affirmed and loved.

Here's a summary of the three basic ways the parents of these teens conveyed affirmation to them.

• One of the most common ways was simply by saying "I love you" early and often. Parents used complimentary notes and gave unexpected small gifts to go along with verbal affirmations. Imagine how the lives of teenagers would change if this message was repeated to all teens. It doesn't need to be the message, "I love you but . . ." with an attachment of a punishment or a restriction. Just saying to the teen, "You are loved, not because of anything you are doing or not doing, but just because you are who you are."

• Many teens stated that these were daily messages of affirmation. Daily interactions are constant reminders of care. The message may be, "You are important to me, so I'm interested in how things are going." A teen can sense when you ask because you care, rather than because you are being nosy or untrusting. Asking about them in a respectful manner affirms their worth as a person.

• Affirmations were not only verbal, but also physical. Teens felt affirmed when a parent showed up for regular events or special occasions.

The Affection Angle

In the *Choosing the Best* survey, 95 percent of our teens said they received affection in these ways:

"Lots of hugs"
"Hugs, kisses and talking"
"Hugs before bed; gifts that say 'I love you'
"Hugs, pats on the back. Dad lets me hold the crook of his arm."
"Cuddle with me and tell me they love me."
" Talk to me; we spend time together."
"My mother kisses me every night before I go to bed and every morning before I go to school. She tells me she loves me all the time."
"Hugs, kisses, positive words; taking care of me."
"Hugs, kisses, cooks me things I like!"

What consistent expressions of affection did you notice in these comments? Certainly they show the importance of hugs and kisses. Parents often think their teens no longer want hugs and kisses and, in fact, hugging a young teen sometimes feels like you're hugging a rigid mannequin. Teens whose bodies are growing often feel self-conscious about face-to-face, full-force hugs. But, our teen experts encourage us parents not to give up.

Appropriate affection can involve more than just a hug. It can be an arm around the shoulder, a pat on the arm, offering an arm while you walk. There are also appropriate times for hugs and kisses. A goodbye smooch in front of the football team is not going to win you points with your teen! But, notice again that the frequency and consistency in the hugs and kisses result in feelings of affection and acceptance. You can combine those hugs and kisses with special acts of kindness for extra boosts of affection.

The Achievement Angle

Achievements can be goals that are reached, or positive actions that contribute to the life of the teen or others. In our *Choosing the Best* survey, 92 percent of abstinent teens identified specific accomplishments they had achieved. That noise you hear in the background is their parents' joyous applause! Some of the achievements they listed included:

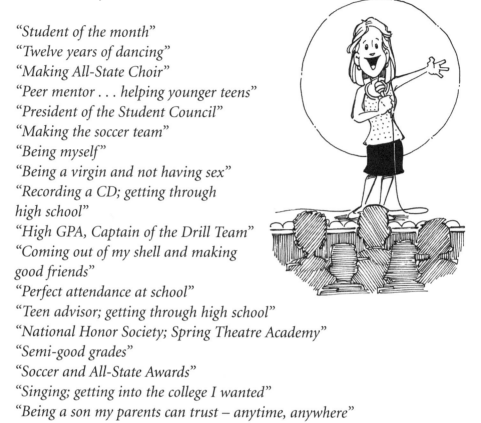

"Student of the month"
"Twelve years of dancing"
"Making All-State Choir"
"Peer mentor . . . helping younger teens"
"President of the Student Council"
"Making the soccer team"
"Being myself"
"Being a virgin and not having sex"
"Recording a CD; getting through
high school"
"High GPA, Captain of the Drill Team"
"Coming out of my shell and making
good friends"
"Perfect attendance at school"
"Teen advisor; getting through high school"
"National Honor Society; Spring Theatre Academy"
"Semi-good grades"
"Soccer and All-State Awards"
"Singing; getting into the college I wanted"
"Being a son my parents can trust – anytime, anywhere"

Aren't these answers wonderful? While their list includes academic, athletic, and extracurricular achievements, several students felt like just surviving high school, making friends, or being abstinent in a sex-crazed society were significant accomplishments. This shows that competency is not in the magnitude of the achievement, but in the process the teen used to reach that achievement. Let's look at that process:

• First, **identify the goal**. The teen decides on what he or she wants to achieve – good grade point average, just passing English Literature and Algebra II, making new friends, making the soccer team.

• Next decide on **what it takes** to reach the goal. What effort must be expended? Sometimes gifted students feel they haven't accomplished anything, even if they achieve good grades or make the team, because they haven't expended any real effort. The gifted student may have to find a challenge that is more difficult – perhaps learning to play a musical instrument, tutoring underprivileged children, learning how to maintain a car.

• Once the goal is set and the smaller steps to reach that goal are determined, there will be **barriers to overcome**. Most goals run into difficulty. Learning to handle disruptions and discouragements are excellent confidence builders.

• Finally, the **goal is reached**. This can be something the teen has done or something the teen has become, such as becoming a trustworthy person, someone who befriends lonely students, and so on.

As you affirm your teen's achievement, don't focus only on the achievement. Consider the effort and the character traits that helped your teen reach that goal. Otherwise, reaching the goal can become so important that your teen will be devastated when there is failure or will be unprepared for the rest of life once the goal is reached. Here are several examples of supporting the person and the goal by acknowledging the effort and character traits inherent within each achievement:

> *"Congratulations on winning the Student Government election! You will bring a balance of honesty and enthusiasm to the office."*

> *"I'm so proud of your grades. I know it took extra work. You really showed determination."*

> *"Thanks for being a trustworthy person upon whom I can count."*

With each "angle" present and balanced in this self-esteem triangle, a teen grows in the ability to overcome self-doubt, to gain confidence, to withstand peer pressure, and to become trustworthy in making healthy decisions. Like all areas of life, building and maintaining self-esteem is an ongoing process that requires nurturing and daily care. Expect times when both you and your teen struggle with feeling good about yourselves. Above all, celebrate the days of affirmation, affection, and achievement.

Parent: Let's Think About It!

Use the following activity to evaluate how you show affection and affirmation to your teen, and how you support your teen's achievements.

1. Make three lists with these headings:
   - Ways I show affection to my teen
   - Ways I show affirmation to my teen
   - Ways I support my teen's achievements

2. Parents tend to parent their children the way they were parented. If your parents weren't very affectionate with you, you may find it difficult to be affectionate with your teen. If your parents expected you to achieve more than you did, then you will tend to have the same high, sometimes unrealistic, expectations. However, you are not your parent; you are a different person from your own parents. You can break the cycle of destructive parenting and work on the three parts to build your teen's self-esteem. Write down a few ideas under each topic:

   - Ways I can strengthen my affirmation of my teen
   - Ways I can strengthen my affection towards my teen
   - Ways I can support the achievements of my teen

   Now circle one or two that you can start working on today.

3. It's hard to help another person develop self-esteem if you don't have feelings of self-worth yourself. Take the Self-Esteem Evaluation Survey, which can be found on the Internet. The survey is self-scoring. It will help you see where your self-esteem can be improved.

Parent and Teen: Let's Talk About It!
Discussion Six – Building Self-Esteem

1. **Self-Esteem.** Self-esteem or self-worth is more than how you feel about yourself. It's also about how capable you are to meet life's challenges and feel worthy of happiness. Personal experiences and relationships with others who mean something to you affect your sense of self-worth. In turn, this affects your decisions and actions. Good self-esteem begins by identifying and appreciating that you are ... **Unique, One-of-a-Kind!**

Parent: Think of something that represents you – a song, a certain animal, a flower, a sport, etc. How does this represent you? _____

_____

(_Example, "I am like a Golden Retriever because I like to please people."_)

Teen: Think of something that represents you – a song, a certain animal, a flower, a sport, etc. How does this represent you? _____

_____

(_Example, "I am like an otter because I like to be playful and have fun."_)

Everyone has one or more abilities. Look at the list below and identify the things you do well. Include other activities you enjoy that are not listed. Teen, use a **T** to mark your responses; parents, use a **P** beside each ability you identify.

Making friends	Good with numbers	Playing sports
Thinking creatively	Making things	Building things
Artistic	Solving problems	Sense of humor
Speaking	Working with others	Making decisions
Writing	Playing a music instrument	Counseling others
Being friendly	Dancing	Accepting others
Singing	Caring for others	Listening
Good with words	_____	_____

2. **Effect of Teen Years on Self-Esteem.** During the teen years, feelings

of doubt and discouragement can bombard the average young person. Identify the situations below that you think can contribute to feelings of low self-worth. Teen, use a **T** to mark your responses; parents, use a **P** beside each situation you identify.

Losing a friend

Not liking your body

Struggling in school

Not making a team/tryout

Feeling unattractive

Not fitting into a group

Not being athletic

Feeling stupid/not smart

Not measuring up to parents' expectations

_____

3. **Building Self-Esteem.** You can build self-esteem by developing three "A's": Affirmation, Achievement and Affection. A triangle of equal sides represents these three aspects of self-esteem. Picture the goal of building self-esteem to be increasing all three sides proportionately. Discuss specific ways each side can be strengthened.

❖ **Affirmation.** Being affirmed means to be valued for who you are (not what you do) by a significant person in your life. Teens with high self-esteem feel affirmed by their parents. Discuss the following questions:

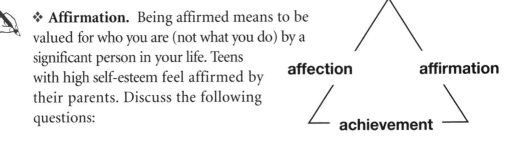

affection   **affirmation**

achievement

◆ **Teen:** How can a parent affirm a teen?

_____

◆ **Parent:** How can a parent affirm a teen?

_____

◆ **Teen and Parent:** Think of a time when you felt affirmed, either by your family or by others in your life. Share the situation and your thoughts and feelings.

◆ **Teen:** Rate your "Affirmation Quotient" – how well do you feel affirmed by your family?

Not At All   Somewhat   Acceptable   Quite A Bit   Awesome

It would help me feel more affirmed if you (my parents) could:

_____

◆ **Parent:** Rate your "Affirmation Quotient" – how well do you feel you affirm your teen?

Not At All   Somewhat   Acceptable   Quite A Bit   Awesome

❖ **Achievement.** Teens with high self-esteem can identify specific accomplishments they have achieved. These teens also feel parental recognition for these achievements.

◆ **Teen:** Identify a specific accomplishment(s) that has given you a sense of satisfaction or made you feel proud

_____

_____

◆ **Parent:** What character qualities and traits did it take for your teen to achieve these accomplishment(s)?

_____

_____

◆ **Teen:** Rate how often you feel you receive recognition from your parent for your accomplishments.

Never   Rarely   Sometimes   Often   Frequently

It would help me feel better about my achievements if you (my parents) could _____

◆ **Parent:** Rate how often you feel you give recognition for your teen's accomplishments.

Never   Rarely   Sometimes   Often   Frequently

❖ **Affection.** Teens with high self-esteem report that their parents frequently show affection to them. Respond to these questions.

◆ **Teen:** How should a parent show affection to a teen?

_____

_____

◆ **Parent:** How could you show affection to your teen?

_____

_____

◆ **Teen and Parent:** Think of a time when you felt affection, either from your family or from others in your life. Share the situation and your thoughts and feelings.

◆ **Teen:** Rate your "Affection Quotient" – how well do you feel affection from your family?

Never   Rarely   Sometimes   Often   Frequently

It would help me feel your (my parents') affection if you would

_____

_____

◆ **Parent:** Rate your "Affection Quotient" – how well do you feel you show affection to your teen?

Never   Rarely   Sometimes   Often   Frequently

4. **Sex and Self-Esteem.** How can sex outside of marriage affect a young person's self-worth? Read what these real-life teens have to say and discuss the questions below.

Lathia: _"The only way to convince him that I loved him was to have sex with him, that day when he wanted it . . . . Being used lowers your self-esteem. It makes you feel like less [of] a woman. You think you're an object of some sort. Going into other new relationships, you put yourself in worse relationships, like abusive relationships."_ [1]

Eldon: _"I thought that if I had sex with her it would totally change the relationship, change how she looked at me. She would have to_ *love me. When I did have sex with her, it didn't change anything. I felt bonded with her, and she didn't feel the same way."* [2]

◆ Why did these teens feel "used"? Why?

◆ Does being abstinent until marriage help or hurt self-esteem? Why?

7

Step Seven

Talk About Relationships

How Do I Know When I'm In Love?

Most teens want this BIG question answered:

How do I know when I am in love?

What if the only answer about relationships between the sexes came from the movies? What conclusions would your teenager draw? Your teen might think relationships develop like this . . .

SCENE 1: The guy and girl meet and instantly are attracted to each other. You know of this attraction because of the way she smiles, the softer look in his eyes, the way he stands a little taller, and the way she leans towards him. And the soft music playing in the background gives it away.

CONCLUSION: When you meet someone of the opposite sex, you will have an immediate attraction to that person.

SCENE 2: The guy and girl fall in love, usually within the first few hours, over the next few days, or at least by the weekend. You know they are in love because they say they are, and their kisses deepen as they caress

one another's bodies. And, of course, the strings in the orchestra grow louder.

CONCLUSION: True love happens quickly, and even if you don't feel anything, saying so makes it happen. Saying you're in love gives you permission to kiss and touch each other all over.

SCENE 3: Once the guy and girl say they're in love, they rip off each other's clothes (usually the girl's clothes come off first), then they have sex.

CONCLUSION: If it's true love, sex happens. Sex is the ultimate expression of true love.

SCENE 4: The guy and girl live together happily ever after. They never worry about any negative consequences of sex without the commitment of marriage, such as pregnancy or STDs. They have no feelings of being used or of guilt and regret. Sex is always beautiful, romantic, fun, and natural.

CONCLUSION: Anytime you feel fuzzy, warm feelings about another person, jump into bed with that person, have sex, wake up, and go on with the rest of your life – or to put it another way: in the movies, SEX equals LOVE.

Unfortunately, with the typical American child consuming more than 38 hours of media (TV, computers, movies, music, and print media) each week,[1] teens can be heavily influenced by the messages they hear. Teens who receive "relationship education" from the media or from our popular culture end up with a distorted view of how close relationships develop. As a result, many teens believe sex always occurs to create a more meaningful relationship between a guy and girl. Unfortunately, many supporters of comprehensive sex education agree that sex is OK when two teens have feelings for each other.

Does Sex Equal Love?
One hundred percent of the teens in our *Choosing the Best* survey, who have committed to abstinence until marriage, stated emphatically that sex does not equal love. Contrary to the pop culture of today, these teens have learned there is a big difference between being in

real love and just having sex. These teen experts received a different kind of relationship education than the media communicates. Their relationship education came from parents who took the time to help them understand how healthy relationships develop and how sex fits into the equation.

When asked to describe what sex outside of marriage looks like, the *Choosing the Best* teens survey respondents expressed it this way:

> *"Physical only"*
> *"Meaningless without love"*
> *"Cheapens sex"*
> *"Lust"*
> *"Self-centered pleasing own needs of self"*

Many of these teens agreed that sex outside of marriage provides a cheapened and inferior version of real love.

What are the key relational principles our teens need to know? Let me suggest four.

Principle #1 – Guys and Girls Are Really Different

These teens describe their relationships with members of the opposite sex. They seem a little confused!

Susan: *"I was always the one [who] was trying to talk about things, and feel things, and communicate. And he never wanted to. And I think that's pretty much a true stereotype about guys. [Communication] is a big problem for a lot of them."* [2]

Matt: *"Guys think about sex so much more than girls, it's beyond belief. I guess that's just the way we are 'cause we have got like testosterone and stuff, and they don't. Guys are horny and most guys will take [sex] anyway that they can get it."* [3]

Katie: *"When you're on a date, it always seems like the guy wants to initiate or start something, you know. Guys need to be careful with sex, because it can be very powerful over the girl's emotions."* [4]

Josh: *"If you're trying to do something, it would be safer to ask. But it's always an uncomfortable situation, because how do you go about asking?"* [5]

Clare: *"Guys can't open up to girls. They can't tell like what they really feel. They just say, like, whatever the girl wants to hear so they can get whatever they want."* [6]

John Gray, in his popular book, *Men Are From Mars and Women Are From Venus*, has developed an awareness of the differences between males and females. His conclusion is that men and women *really* are different. We don't naturally understand each other's differences. One explanation for this comes from researchers who have discovered that females have more connective tissue between the right and left parts of the brain. This allows women to have simultaneous access to the right side of the brain (feelings and emotions) and the left side (concrete thinking and reasoning). Girls process things in "stereo." It's not just thoughts about the situation or event, but it's thoughts surrounded by emotion and feelings. Guys, however, are more focused, accessing one side of the brain at a time.

How does this affect "relationship building" with members of the opposite sex? Take the male sex hormone testosterone, which produces intense sexual surges four or five times a day in the average teen guy. Couple it with a brain that focuses on one item at a time. Now, you have guys who can view sex as separate from an emotional relationship. Girls, on the other hand, with their "stereo" view of life, tend to view sex as part of an overall relationship.

What's the solution to helping teens understand the differences in guys and girls? In one exercise in *Choosing the Best* **PATH**, our sex education program for middle schoolers, the leader divides guys and girls into separate groups. Each group has to come up with responses relating to what qualities they look for in someone of the opposite sex, what qualities make a great date, and what activities make a great date. As the young teens share their answers, communication between genders occurs, and eyes begin to open. Understanding the differences in guys and girls can help build communication with those of the opposite sex.

Principle #2 – Crushes, Infatuation, and Love Are Different

Teens tend to experience three different kinds of "love" relationships as they mature into adulthood. Because of intense feelings, powerful hormones, and the newness of relating to the opposite sex, confusion about "being in love" is rampant in teen relationships. In fact, in one survey, 85 percent of eighth-grade boys say they already have been in a real love relationship.

Let's explore the differences among these three basic relationships – a crush, infatuation, and real love, using the analogies of a regular balloon, a helium-filled balloon, and a basketball.

A Crush – POP! Crushes are characterized by intense feelings that some teens mistake for real love. In reality, those feelings are just hormones kicking in. Just as the brain triggers the release of hormones to start the process of puberty, it also reacts to these same hormones. These hormones flip neurological switches to produce intense feelings of pleasure, new emotions, the ability to judge, and impulse control.

A crush is a sudden attraction to someone of the opposite sex. Usually the attraction occurs because of a physical feature. A crush is like a balloon, which filled with air takes on a new shape and quickly becomes buoyant. The balloon, however, is vulnerable to the slightest pinprick. Like a burst balloon, a crush can end just as suddenly as it began, sometimes over a trivial matter. Crushes can happen frequently during the teen years. Crushes feel like love, but they are not love.

Infatuation – INFLATED! Infatuation soars like an inflated helium balloon. A helium balloon rises higher and stays up longer than a regular balloon. A crush can evolve into infatuation. Unfortunately, infatuation is mostly selfish love. Infatuation asks, "How do I feel?" "Will she like me?" "What will I say?" "What will I wear?" Sometimes infatuation develops deep feelings, some of which can be negative, such as feelings of jealousy or anger. In an infatuation, each person may try to hold the string and tend to be possessive of the other person's time and friendship.

Like a helium balloon that slowly deflates over time and sinks to the floor, a relationship built on infatuation lasts longer than a crush but eventually "sinks." It cannot sustain itself because infatuation is a love untested by a variety of situations. It is not uncommon for young people to be infatuated with several people. Infatuation can grow into love, but it is not love.

In crushes and infatuations, hormonal feelings dominate the relationship. One or both people are consumed with thoughts of the other person. They want to be with each other all the time. They can't stand being apart. Sometimes this is called "puppy love" because it is similar to how a puppy reacts in showing affection towards its owner. This shallow type of love either fades over time or can be the starting point of a more mature, self-giving love.

Love – LONG-LASTING! Real love is like a basketball. Air inflates the basketball just as it did both balloons. However, the tough hide on the outside of the basketball represents a stronger commitment to each other. The pinpricks of real life don't destroy this relationship because a strong commitment protects the relationship. This time, the relationship is built on an intense desire to tend to and care for the other person. This love is not

selfish, but giving. Real love wants the best for the other person. Real love is considerate and kind. It does not demand, control, or misuse the other person. Real love makes a commitment to the well-being of the other person.

Even though there are some challenges in a real love relationship, like the basketball, this love bounces back as the two people work to keep their commitment to one another intact. Through problems and struggles, real love is tested by time, and it lasts. True love happens very few times in a person's life. This love grows with time and survives various circumstances.

How does a person know if the feeling is infatuation or love? True love is tested by time! Love can be as passionate and intense as infatuation. Over time, the strength of that passion will ebb and flow again, but the difference is that love survives times of struggle and trials. As new relationships, challenging events and life-altering situations occur, the shallowness of an infatuation won't last. Real love, however, is grounded in commitment and a willingness to care for the other person. With time, love grows and matures, offering stability and security to both people.

Here's how several mature *Choosing the Best* teen experts describe the love relationship that leads to marriage:

> *"Caring for someone; being there"*
> *"Responsibility and commitment"*
> *"Waiting and respecting"*
> *"Doing the best for the other person, not self-centered"*

Older teens are capable of experiencing real love. While parents may dismiss all teen relationships as infatuations or puppy love, they should know that even casual relationships create feelings of betrayal, grief, and pain when the relationship ends. Heightened by the teen's normal, vacillating emotional state, parents need to be sympathetic and understanding, rather than judgmental or impatient. Comments of support, such as "I know you really care for him," are more helpful than comments like: "You'll get over it!" or "I knew it wouldn't last."

or "Why are you so upset?" Try to remember how you felt when the relationships of your youth ended. The pain and grief were real.

Principle #3 – Avoid Unhealthy Relationships

Relationships are tied closely to emotional needs. Just as our bodies require air, food, rest, water, and other physical needs, we also require emotional support, such as love, acceptance, security, and value. When teens' emotional needs are met by support and encouragement from their families and other healthy sources, they won't need to look in unhealthy places. When teens don't feel loved, safe, accepted, or valued, they turn to unhealthy relationships. Many of these unhealthy relationships can develop into sexual experiences. These two young people explain their unhealthy relationships.

> **Jackie:** *"Sex definitely was the way that I would feel more desirable and older. [It] felt good that someone actually wanted me around. Guys would tell me ['You're] beautiful; I love you.' Their motives were more, 'I want to have sex with you' instead of 'I really love you.'"* [7]

> **Eldon:** *"I wanted to belong to somebody. [There was] this part of me that wanted to be loved by somebody, because at the time I wasn't getting it from my family. I feel like, you know when I get into a relationship too early, and I catch feelings early, I put my heart on the line. It puts me out there to get hurt."* [8]

In ***Choosing the Best* WAY**, the curriculum designed for sixth graders, we ask the kids to think of themselves with empty emotional tanks. Healthy relationships fill their emotional tanks with positive, healthy emotional needs – love, acceptance, being valued, feeling safe, having self-confidence. So when mom hugs her teen, love is added to his tank. When the teacher tells a teen how proud he is of the teen's hard work, self-confidence is added to the emotional tank. When a coach recognizes a teen's hard work,

the emotional tank gets filled with acceptance and pride. Unhealthy relationships drain away the healthy needs, and fill their emotional tanks with unhealthy emotions. When someone uses a teen to meet his personal physical needs, the teen feels used. When a friend pushes a teen to go beyond a personal boundary, the teen feels pressured and confused. When a teen is pressured to have sex, the emotional tank is emptied of self-esteem.

Principle #4 – Relationships That Develop Without Sex Are Stronger

For many teens, when sex is introduced into the relationship, it can easily become the main focus. Instead of developing the deeper parts of a meaningful relationship – trust, communication, shared values, common interests – sex can short-circuit the relationship-building process. An orchestra is tuned from the most sensitive instrument first, the violin. The other instruments, woodwinds and brass follow in order. Last are the bass drums. When sex enters a relationship outside of marriage, it's like tuning your "relationship orchestra" beginning with the bass drum.

Studies in the *Journal of Marriage and the Family* found that couples who cohabitate (live together before marriage) have less stable marriages than those in which sex begins with marriage. One study found that for each 100 couples who are sexually active and live together prior to marriage, 40 will break up before marriage; of the remaining 60 who marry, 45 will divorce, leaving only 15 intact marriages.[9]

Sex outside of marriage raises concerns about trustworthiness and fidelity. And of course, sex outside of marriage always brings with it the risks mentioned earlier – emotional risks, pregnancy risk, and disease risks, any of which can work to erode the basis of a meaningful and lasting relationship.

Meaningful Teen Relationships Without Sex

Let's listen to two real-life older teens talk about their relationships:

> **Melody:** *"Now I'm dating Darin and he and I both made the decision to abstain and so it's really worked out well. It's kind of neat having someone else there that understands and respects your wishes and*

wants the best thing for himself. He's my best friend and that's the neat part about our relationship."

Darin: *"I trust and respect Melody very much and if we're ever doing something that she feels is uncomfortable, I don't hesitate to get out of the situation and say that's fine with me. We know when to draw the line, and I don't want to push her to do anything she doesn't want to do . . . There are a lot of things you can do. Because people think if you're intimate, you have to be having sex, but that's not true. I mean, we kiss and stuff, and we can have a nice dinner together holding hands. I like going to the beach and just cuddling on the beach, just holding each other on the beach, watching the sunset or something like that. You can do a lot of things that aren't sex – you don't have to have sex to be intimate."* [10]

What would you say about this relationship? Sounds like the "relationship orchestra" is being tuned with the violin and not the bass drum. The foundations are being developed for a growing and long-lasting relationship.

The Real Value of Sex – One teen put it this way: "The gift of virginity can only be unwrapped once."[11] Sex is intended as a wonderful gift, an expression of a love relationship that within the context of marriage is the ultimate way to share personal intimacy. That's why surveys of faithfully married couples show more sexual pleasure and emotional satisfaction when compared to those who are not married.[12] The emotional and physical part of a relationship is protected through the security and trust of commitment.

It's too easy to get caught up in emotional feelings and think that's what real love involves. Help your teen sort out the feelings as you discuss the differences in the "Let's Talk About It" Discussion section. Teens can learn that sex does not create love, and that love does not require sex.

Parent: Let's Think About It!

Before talking with your teen, think about the following questions. Later, you can share your thoughts with your teen.

1. What do you remember about your first crush? How long did it last? When did you know it was over?

2. Have you ever been infatuated with someone? What was that like? Did your infatuation end or grow into love? How did that occur?

3. How did you know when you were in love? What feelings and events confirmed that you were in love?

4. Consider the wedding vows used at many ceremonies: "for better, for worse; in sickness and in health; for richer, for poorer; to love and to cherish till death do us part."

   (a) On a sheet of paper, draw a time line of your love life. Include things like your first crush, your first kiss, when you met your teen's other parent, the highs and lows in the love of your marriage. Identify "for better, for worse" events that have strained the love and times that have strengthened that love.

   (b) What did you learn about love from this exercise?

   (c) How would you feel about sharing this love line, or parts of it, with your teen?

As you get ready to talk with your teen using the activities in the Discussion section, remember that some teens may not be ready to talk about love and marriage, especially younger teen boys. But you can use these exercises at any time with your teen. The idea is to keep the communication lines open. So, choose the activities and exercises that best fit your situation.

Parent and Teen: Let's Talk About It!
Discussion Seven – Relationships

1. **"Relationship Building" in Four Scenes.** Read the following message from the movies about how relationships develop. Then, respond to the questions below.

> SCENE 1: The guy and girl meet and instantly are attracted to each other. You know of this attraction because of the way she smiles, the softer look in his eyes, the way he stands a little taller, and the way she leans towards him. And the soft music playing in the background gives it away.
>
> SCENE 2: The guy and girl fall in love, usually within the first few hours, over the next few days, or at least by the weekend. You know they are in love because they say they are, and their kisses deepen as they caress one another's bodies. And, of course, the strings in the orchestra grow louder.
>
> SCENE 3: Once the guy and girl say they're in love, they rip off each other's clothes (usually the girl's clothes come off first), then they have sex.
>
> SCENE 4: The guy and girl live together happily ever after. They never worry about any negative consequences of sex without the commitment of marriage, such as pregnancy or STDs. They have no feelings of being used or of guilt and regret. Sex is always beautiful, romantic, fun, and natural.

What conclusions would you make about relationships if this were your only source of information?

Teen: Do you agree or disagree with this view of how relationships are formed? Why or why not?

Parent: Do you agree or disagree with this view of how relationships are formed? Why or why not?

2. **Does Love Equal Sex?** Read the following comments from real–life teens. For each conclusion below the comment, discuss and indicate whether you agree or disagree.

"A lot of times, my friends will tell me they had sex with their boyfriends because they said, "If you love me, you'll have sex with me."" [1]
Conclusion: Sometimes people believe that sex and love are the same thing.
❏ Agree   ❏ Disagree

"If a guy wants to have sex with a girl, he would say: 'I love you' just to have sex and afterwards he's gone." [2]
Conclusion: Sometimes guys will make statements about love to get sex, and girls will use sex to get "love."
❏ Agree   ❏ Disagree

"You can be in an awesome relationship and not have to worry about sex at all, because I'm in one now, and I love it without sex." [3]
Conclusion: Relationships that develop without sex are stronger.
❏ Agree   ❏ Disagree

"You can still love someone and show your love without having to have sex." [4]
Conclusion: There are many ways you can show your love without having sex.
❏ Agree   ❏ Disagree

3. **Three Types of Relationships: Crushes, Infatuation, and Love.** Read a description of three different types of relationships. Discuss and then identify all the qualities that you think explain each type of relationship.

❖ **Crush.** Crushes are like balloons. They can be quickly inflated and continue to expand, but the slightest pinprick can burst the balloon.

Crushes:

❏ Are sudden attractions to someone of the opposite sex.
❏ Happen quickly.
❏ Are characterized by intense feelings.
❏ End quickly – sometimes over a trivial matter.
❏ Are enough upon which to build a sexual relationship.

Parent: Did you ever have any crushes? How did you feel when they ended?

❖ **An Infatuation.** Infatuations are like helium-filled balloons. They rise higher than regular balloons and stay up longer. However, over time, the helium leaks out of the balloon, and it slowly sinks to the floor. Infatuations:

❏ Also begin with intense feelings.
❏ Can be very possessive, with one person holding the string.
❏ Focus on "How I feel?"
❏ Will break up over time.
❏ Are enough upon which to build a sexual relationship.

Parent: Did you ever have any serious infatuation relationships? How did you know whether or not these were real love?

❖ **Real Love.** Real love is like a basketball. Just like balloons, air is needed to inflate the basketball. However, the tough outside of the basketball protects it from pinpricks and leakage, enabling couples to bounce back in their commitment to each other. Real love:

❏ Develops over time.
❏ Is long-lasting.
❏ Is based on a commitment to the well-being of the other person.
❏ Is giving, considerate, kind and does not demand, control or misuse the other person.
❏ Is enough upon which to build a sexual relationship within a marriage.

Parent: How did you know when you were in love?

(Want to know the answers? All of the checkboxes for Crushes and Infatuations should be checked EXCEPT the last one about a sexual relationship. All of the boxes for Real Love should be checked. How did you do?)

4. **Unhealthy Relationships.** Healthy relationships fill our emotional tanks with positive, healthy emotions of love, acceptance, being valued and feeling safe. However, unhealthy relationship can cause someone to feel "used" and less valued.

◆ What are the signs of unhealthy relationships?

_____

◆ What are the signs of healthy relationships?

_____

◆ How can you avoid unhealthy relationships?

_____

◆ How can you cultivate healthy relationships?

_____

8

Step Eight

Establish Rules and Boundaries

Freedom Within Boundaries

"Let Me Out of Here! Oh No! Put Me Back!"
One exercise from *Choosing the Best* **PATH**, the curriculum designed for middle school students, involves the teacher bringing to class a live goldfish in a bowl. The teaching experience happens like this:

> The teacher explains: *"Everyday, George the Goldfish peers out of his bowl and wonders what it would be like to be free from his glass prison. He dreams of being able to go where he wants to go when he wants, and of not being confined to the limited space of the fish bowl. Well, today I'm going to make George's dream come true."*

Using a fish net, the leader scoops George out of his prison and frees him by placing the fish on the desk. George desperately flops around, realizing that freedom may cost him his life. Students typically protest the teacher's action and loudly demand that George be returned to the fish bowl before it's too late.

After reminding the students that George asked to be removed from the restrictions of his boundaries within the bowl, the teacher returns George to the safety and comfort of his fish bowl. Upon his return, George relaxes and resumes his casual swimming around in the freedom of his bowl.

The discussion that follows this exercise provides remarkable insight for teens as to why boundaries are needed. Suddenly, instead of viewing boundaries and rules as restrictive, they see firsthand how healthy boundaries provide freedom. Positive, healthy boundaries allow teens freedom to pursue their dreams and goals, and to be protected from the fear of pregnancy, STDs and broken hearts.

In fact, psychologists tell us that adolescents need rules and boundaries. Left by themselves to figure out what to do and where to go, teens become frustrated, usually reverting to at-risk behaviors. But when a parent or guardian specifically states, "This is how far to go. You cannot do this. Here are the limits. This the appropriate behavior I expect from you," the teen has a glass bowl or a safety net for protection. Attention to rules

In the largest survey of adolescents ever conducted in the United States, public health experts discovered that teens want more structure. Robert W. Blum, M.D., Ph.D., professor of pediatrics at the University of Minnesota and the study's lead investigator, says, "Too many kids – rich and poor – are left to their own devices. Kids need structure to grow and to be healthy."[1]

and boundaries communicates to a teen that a parent cares. Without those rules and boundaries, a teen can unconsciously become involved in at-risk behaviors to see if the parent is paying attention.

A Wake-Up Call for Parents

To illustrate the devastating effect upon teens who receive few, if any, rules or boundaries from their parents, let's look again at the PBS *Frontline* documentary "The Lost Children of Rockdale County" that you read about in Step Five. This was a story of sexual activity among more than 200 teenagers in an upscale suburban community.

Now let's focus on the story of Steve and Catherine, parents of five children, one of whom is Kevin, a teenage son. Kevin's family lived in house in back of the house. Let's hear from Kevin, his sister Jenny, Catherine (the mother) and Steve (the father).

Kevin: *"Most people, when they're 17, their parents won't let them stay out as long as they want. I come and go whenever I want. They're not really the kind of parents to really give a lot of discipline."*

Jenny: *(Kevin's 19-year-old sister): "They used to be real strict on us. It was like, us kids kind of took over and started to do what we wanted to, and they just gave up."*

Here's what discipline was like in Kevin and Jenny's house:

Catherine: *(Kevin's mother): "I think you should, you know, put your foot down and tell them that you're not going to put up with this and that. Just the other day, me and Jenny [were] talking, and she said, 'I wish you had been more strict with me.' I said, 'Jenny, how could I – you wouldn't let me be strict. You threatened to run away. That's easy for you to say now, but the child you are, stubborn as you are, how could I have been stricter with you?'"*

Steve: *(Kevin's father): "[Catherine] disagrees with me, but my feeling is you need to give them a little bit of leeway. Let them go out and sow their oats as they're young, so they won't do it when they're old. Put them on a long leash."*

Catherine: *"Yeah. I literally gave up. I got tired of the fighting, the bickering with Jenny. My nerves would be shot. And I got to the point where it's easier for me to let Jenny go do what she wants to instead of standing there fussing and fighting with her. And we get along better . . . The struggle is over."*

Sounds modern and enlightened, doesn't it? Here's a teenage son with his own place in which to live who comes and goes as he chooses. Add a daughter who gets her way simply by arguing long enough. Don't forget the mother who is concerned, but who has abdicated her responsibility because she's tired of fighting. Then there's the father who excuses his children's behavior because "boys will be boys." Both mom and dad have abdicated their roles as parents for false peace and harmony in the family. How did their teenagers respond to their enlightened approach? What was the resulting effect on Kevin?

> *"[I'd go to] a party of like 200 people. Everybody'd get drunk, spend the night, swim in the pool. There was a lot of sex going on then. Like, one girl would come in the group and she'd be passed around, or one guy would go in the girl's group and get passed around."*

Then, came the trip to Panama City, Florida.

> *"Everything got crazy. We stayed drunk the whole time. Everywhere people were fighting, busting bottles over people's heads. I don't know why we were all fighting. We just were."*

Kevin's best friend Keith took off in his Jeep and headed home from Panama City Beach late one night. He never made it. Keith died from the injuries he sustained in a car crash that early spring morning. Still, Kevin's family failed to set boundaries.

> **Kevin:** *"In my family, you're going to do as you want to do. If they tell you to do something, it doesn't matter. You're going to do what you want to do. There's nobody going to stop you - so that's what got me in trouble."* [2]

The freedom that both Kevin and Jenny desired turned out to be an empty victory. Looking back, both acknowledge the desire for rules and boundaries that should have been set by parents who wouldn't give up.

Set Rules While Making Great Relationships

Many parents ask, "How do I set rules and hang on to them during my kid's teen years?" Catherine and Steve had rules when their children were younger, only to give up in a battle of wills during the teen years. The answer to disciplining teens and hanging onto relationships with them can be found in three foundational parenting truths:

> 1. *Rules without Relationship Produce Rebellion.*
> 2. *Relationship without Rules Produces Promiscuity.*
> 3. *Rules with Relationship Produce Effective Parenting.*

Considering these three points, how strong was the relationship level in Kevin's house? Catherine shares this insight:

"We've never been a family where we hugged, you know. We don't show emotion like that – and we still don't." [3]

Perhaps a starting point for Catherine and Steve would be to develop a relationship with their kids. This involves a genuine communication of love and caring, including lots of hugs, so the teens get the message that they are special and significant. Without a relationship, functioning only on rules moves the teenager into the "rebellion battle," which is very difficult for parents to handle.

A warm, friendly relationship with no rules, however, fails to provide what teens need. Rules and boundaries provide true freedom. As Beth Ross, the director of counseling for Rockdale County Schools pointed out about "The Lost Children of Rockdale County":

"No one has ever sat down and specifically said to [these teens], 'This is how far you go. This is the limit' that 'This is what I will accept from you as appropriate.' The anxiety of not having the limits on a regular basis can be extremely debilitating to the child." [4]

Ten Rules That Bring Freedom

Here are 10 rules or boundaries that can bring freedom to the life of your teenager, like the goldfish bowl did for George. Set rules with these basics in mind:

- Adjust the rules to fit the age of your teenager.
- Involve your teenager in the process of setting the rules.
- Review the rules every six months, making adjustments based on your ability to trust your teen and the teen's responsibility in keeping the rules.
- Model for your teen personal boundaries set in your life.

• As your teen gets older, look for ways to give the teenager a chance to set his own boundaries. This is a crucial step. If you make all the rules, demand strict obedience, and punish the slightest infraction, you fail to produce a teen who knows how to set personal boundaries. When your teen goes to college or gets a job,

10 Rules That Bring Freedom

Freedom Rule #1 - Wait to Date

Freedom Rule #2 - Age Differences Matter

Freedom Rule #3 - No "Home-Alone" Visitors

Freedom Rule #4 - Be Home on Time

Freedom Rule #5 - Avoid Alcohol and Drugs

Freedom Rule #6 - Avoid "At-Risk" Situations

Freedom Rule #7 - Watch What You Watch

Freedom Rule #8 - Screen the 'Net

Freedom Rule #9 - Tame the Tunes

Freedom Rule #10 - Set Personal Boundaries

there are no boundaries. Use these "10 Rules That Bring Freedom" as a starting point.

Freedom Rule #1 – Wait to Date

Avoid letting your young teen jump into the dating scene too early. Research has linked the age of the first date to the age of first intercourse. Of those teens who begin dating before the age of 12 years, 91 percent become sexually active by the end of high school. By delaying dating just one year, until age 13, that percentage decreases to 56 percent.[5] Encourage your teen to participate in activities with a group of friends in the early teen years. Make your home available

for your teenager to bring in friends. Be prepared to suggest a list of fun activities that your teenager can do with a group of friends.

Freedom Rule #2 – Age Differences Matter

An age difference of two years or more between two opposite-sex young people creates a risk factor. Since teens report becoming sexually active as they get older, there is a greater risk for younger girls who date older guys.[6] One survey showed that girls under 16 had their first sexual encounter with a boy two years older more than twice as often as with boys their own age.[7] Encourage your teen to keep the dating age range under two years.

Freedom Rule #3 – No "Home-Alone" Visitors

Teens report that nearly 70 percent of their first sexual experiences happen in the home of one of the teens, either at their home, their partner's home, or at a friend's house.[8] In "The Lost Children of Rockdale County," Beth Ross, director of counseling for Rockdale County Schools reports,

> *"The activities they [the 200 teenagers featured in the study] were involved in, whether it would be sexual or otherwise, the majority of their behavior was taking place between right after school and right before parents came home from work."* [9]

Designate times when you will be home during which it is acceptable for your teen's friends to come to your home.

Freedom Rule #4 – Be Home On Time

Having age-appropriate curfews is a necessary part of providing protection to your teen. The later the hour at night, the more out-of-control events and activities take place. Many cities have curfews for teens. Check to see if your city's curfew can help you set this boundary. As the teen gets older, be willing to negotiate this curfew time, especially if he or she works.

Freedom Rule #5 – Avoid Alcohol and Drugs

Besides the damage that alcohol can do to developing minds and bodies, the consumption of alcohol by minors is illegal in every state of

the Union. In addition, since alcohol lowers inhibitions, the results are those actions that teens later regret. Teens need to know the dangers of alcohol consumption and the significant risk of binge drinking (drinking four or more drinks rapidly in one sitting). Include in this rule that your teen not ride in a car with anyone who has been drinking. This is one of those times when you tell your teen to call you, at anytime from anywhere, and you will pick your teen up NO QUESTIONS ASKED. You must be willing to stick to that last part, as it may save your teen's life.

Freedom Rule #6 – Avoid "At-Risk" Situations

In the teen world, anything can happen at anytime. Relatively tame parties can deteriorate into drunken orgies, especially without adult supervision. Talk with your teen about situations in which teens might engage in at-risk behavior such as sex, alcohol or drugs. For example, discuss the risks of hanging out in a park or in a mall parking lot after hours or riding around (cruising). Young teens are particularly vulnerable because they ask others for rides, and because they may not recognize that a situation is getting out of hand. Again, offer to pick up your teenager at anytime in any place, no questions asked. Tell your teen that another way to get out of a tight situation is to blame you, the parent. Tell the teen it's OK to say: "My mom says I have to be in by 9 o'clock tonight or I'm grounded." "My dad will kill me if he finds me cruising. You'd better drop me off here."

Freedom Rule #7 – Watch What You Watch

Sexually explicit pictures and movies teach a teen an unhealthy and unrealistic view of sex, especially of females. Developing minds can be significantly impaired by sexually explicit material. Remember the principle: Garbage in – garbage out! Be aware of what you bring into the home in magazines, videos and books. Your teens will also be watching what you watch, so here's a time when you can teach discernment. Help your teen learn how to evaluate what is pornographic, what is detrimental, what is garbage. You will not always be around to screen their TV programs, movies, and magazines, so teach them how to do this themselves.

Freedom Rule #8 – Screen the 'Net

The Internet is a great source of information – good and bad. Your teen's use, or abuse, of the Internet should be monitored. Just as you would never let a stranger in your house to visit your teen's room, so you should provide adult supervision of the "strangers" waiting to visit your teen in chat rooms and through offensive Web sites. Clear expectations should be set about sexually explicit sites and chat rooms. Here again, teaching your teen to be discerning is the key. Ask questions like:"What's the purpose of this site? What values does it teach?" If your teen has a computer in her room, tell her that the door must remain open while she's on the Internet. Walk by her room frequently. Or, better yet, place the computer in a common location (the den, a kitchen desk, an open office area) where it can be seen and used by all family members.

Freedom Rule #9 – Tame the Tunes

Music has such an impact in our lives because it speaks to our emotions. Music has the capability of shaping teen hairstyles, clothing, even language. In some cases, music helps a teenager define reality by identifying buried emotions, addressing questions they have, and expressing common feelings and events. Think about the ideas of love, sex, the world, perhaps your religious values, that were shaped by the music you listened to. Unfortunately, some of today's music has sexually explicit lyrics that pervert the role of sex and the way females are viewed. Walt Mueller in *Understanding Today's Youth Culture* lists these prominent themes of some of today's music: sexual promiscuity, sexual perversion, violence, sexual violence, substance abuse, the occult, rebellion, a negative view of the family, materialism, and hopelessness.[10] Which of these values do you want your teen to learn? Teach your teen to choose his or her music wisely, and help them learn to evaluate music. Frequently ask to listen to what your teen is listening to. As part of this rule, include the programs your teen watches on MTV and what concerts he attends.

Freedom Rule #10 – Set Personal Boundaries

You give your teenager a gift when you take the time teach him or her to set personal boundaries. You've just read about the need to set personal boundaries about what the teen sees, reads, hears and does. Remind your teen that within these boundaries, there is great freedom to see, read, hear and do many other activities. The most personal boundary a teen can set is how far to go sexually. This boundary has to be set BEFORE the teen gets into a dating situation. In *Choosing the Best PATH*, this case study illustrates "The Law of Diminishing Returns: you always want more."

The Law Of Diminishing Returns: "You always want more!"

On their first date, Alan and Susie were both shy. As the night went on, they felt more comfortable and held hands. At the end of the date, Alan gave Susie a short good night kiss. On the next date, one kiss was not enough. Alan kissed Susie continuously for several minutes. Eventually, that was no longer satisfying. Deep kissing entered the scene, then bodily caressing, then "other stuff." Before Alan and Susie knew what had happened, they had sexual intercourse, because there was nothing left to satisfy their desires. Soon their relationship grew bitter, and they broke up, each feeling used, insufficient and empty.

In the Discussion section following this chapter, your teen will be asked to draw a line on how far to go on a date. The progression looks like this:

SEXUAL PROGRESSION

Holding hands

Hugging

Kissing

Deep kissing

Bodily caressing

Outercourse

Oral sex

Intercourse

Use the Discussion section to talk through these rules that bring freedom. Getting your teen to buy into these rules is extremely important. Be willing to be flexible and use the rules to respond to reasonable requests from your teen.

What Happens When Rules Are Broken?

What goes through your mind when you see a sign that reads: "Wet paint! Don't touch!"? Do you reach out to test if it's still wet? Something in each of us wants to test a rule or boundary. Your teen is no different.

Expect rules to be tested and, in some cases, broken. Part of the reason for testing is to measure your commitment to the rules. Rules only work if they are enforced. A classic mistake is to state a rule, have it broken, and do nothing. Your teen hears this message loud and clear: *Rules don't matter!* Another classic mistake is to put off the punishment until the next time by saying, "If I catch you doing this again, I'm gonna throw the book at you!" And, I knew I was in trouble as soon as I said this classic line, "You're grounded for life!" Be reasonable in the punishment.

The best way to handle broken rules is to state a consequence at the time you make the rule. As you discuss the 10 Freedom Rules with your teen, discuss a reasonable punishment for infractions. Invite your teen to suggest ideas. Some of my most creative consequences came from my children as they suggested punishments. After several missed curfews and several bouts of nagging, I decided to raise the issue in a family meeting and asked both kids to come up with an appropriate consequence. My son Brannon suggested that for every curfew missed, the time be moved up so the curfew came 30 minutes earlier. The curfew could only be restored to its original time if either of them came in on time at the new curfew time. Another way of handling broken rules is through natural consequences. You'll have a chance to learn more about natural consequences in Step Ten.

Finally, write the rules and consequences down. Post them in a place where you and your teen can see them easily. Written consequences leave little room for arguments.

Parent: Let's Think About It!

We tend to parent in the same way we were parented. If you thought you turned out OK, you may be using the same parenting methods with your teenager. But, if you don't feel like your parents did a good job, don't give up. You are not doomed to repeat the mistakes your parents made with you! The following exercise will help you evaluate your past, as well as your present rules and relationships.

1. As a teenager I was (a) a model child; (b) a flagrant rebel; (c) always breaking the rules, but never getting caught; (d) always breaking the rules and frequently getting caught; (e) (add your own description)

   _____.

2. As a teenager my parents (a) never gave me any guidance about sex and dating; (b) had numerous rules about sex and dating that were strictly enforced; (c) had rules about sex and dating that were not enforced; (d) had rules about sex and dating that didn't relate to my problems at the time.

3. As a teenager, the rule that was the most unreasonable to me was (fill in the blank)

   _____.

4. My parent's parenting style was (a) rules with no relationships between us as a family; (b) lots of good relationships with no identifiable rules; (c) rules that were balanced by healthy family relationships.

5. As a result, when I was a teenager I said to myself "When I get to be the parent of a teenager, I'll never ..." (fill in the blank)

   _____.

6. My teenager is (a) a model child; (b) a flagrant rebel; (c) always breaking the rules, but never getting caught; (d) always breaking the rules and frequently getting caught; (e) (add your own description)

   _____.

7. My parenting style is (a) rules with no relationships between us as a family; (b) lots of good relationships with no identifiable rules; (c) rules that are balanced by healthy family relationships.

8. Of the 10 Freedom Rules presented in this Step, the ones that go along with rules I've established with my teen are (place a check by those that match):
   ❏ 1 - Wait to Date
   ❏ 2 - Age Differences Matter
   ❏ 3 - No "Home-Alone" Visitors
   ❏ 4 - Be Home on Time
   ❏ 5 - Avoid Alcohol and Drugs
   ❏ 6 - Avoid "At-Risk" Situations
   ❏ 7 - Watch What You Watch
   ❏ 8 - Screen the 'Net
   ❏ 9 - Tame the Tunes
   ❏ 10 - Set Personal Boundaries

   Circle those Freedom Rules that you'd like to include with your teen.

9. When my teenager breaks a rule, I feel . . . ; I say . . . ; I do . . . (Write your thoughts on a separate sheet of paper).

10. The most effective punishment when my teen breaks a rule is (fill in the blank)

   _____.

Parent and Teen: Let's Talk About It!
Discussion Eight – Freedom within Boundaries

1. **"Let Me Out of Here! Oh No! Put Me Back!"** Meet George the goldfish. (Pretty corny – but stay with me. George's story makes a good point.) After reading George's story, discuss the questions following it.

George: *"Every day I would peer out of my bowl, wondering what it was like to be free from this glass prison. I dreamed of being able to go where I wanted to go when I wanted to, of not being confined to the limited space of the fish bowl. I wanted to get out so badly that I put an ad in the Free Willy Flyer.*

"One day someone took me up on my offer. Using a specially designed device for freeing fish, the person scooped me out of that fishbowl. At last, freedom! It didn't take long to realize that freedom's not all it's cracked up to be! I desperately flopped around, screaming at the top of my lungs (which is hard to do when you only have gills) "Put me back! Put be back!" I realized that too much freedom would cost me my life. Finally, I was returned to the fish bowl, and none too soon, I might add. Here in the safety and comfort of my fish bowl I now see I have lots of freedom. I can swim, eat, jump around, and breathe in fish breaths. I've learned my lesson – the wrong kind of freedom isn't worth it!"

◆ How is a glass bowl like a set of rules or boundaries to ensure a teen's safety?

◆ How can setting boundaries bring freedom?

♦ What are some boundaries that adults must live with? (Hint: driving laws, getting to work on time, things like that.)

♦ How can going beyond the boundaries or rules set by parents result in severe consequences? Give two or three examples.

_____

_____

_____

2. **Freedom Rules!** In the following activity, look at each rule/boundary and its brief explanation, then answer the related questions. This is a good time to negotiate rules. Teen, be realistic. Parent, be flexible.

❖ **Freedom Rule #1 – Wait to Date.** Dating at an early age tends to lead to sexual activity.

♦ Why do you think this is the case?

_____

♦ How does this rule help protect you?

_____

♦ What other options are there until you are old enough to date?

_____

♦ Write out your Freedom Rule for when to begin dating?

_____

❖ **Freedom Rule #2 – Age Differences Matter.** An age difference of two or more years between two teens of the opposite sex can create a risk factor.

♦ Why do you think this is the case?

_____

_____

_____

♦ How does this rule help protect you?

_____

♦ Write out your Freedom Rule that relates to the idea of age differences. _____

_____

❖ **Freedom Rule #3 – No "Home-Alone" Visitors.** This rule involves your not having a friend of the opposite sex in the home when no adult is present and includes your avoidance of a friend's home when no adult is present. Teens report that nearly 70 percent of their first sexual experiences happen in the home of one of the teens, either at their home, their partner's home, or at a friend's house.[1]

♦ Why do you think this is the case? _____

_____

♦ How does this rule protect you? _____

_____

♦ What freedoms or benefits does this rule give you? _____

_____

♦ This rule gives me the freedom to say no when someone asks to come over.   ❏ Agree   ❏ Disagree

♦ Write out your Freedom Rule that relates to the idea of being home alone. _____

_____

❖ **Freedom Rule #4 – Be Home on Time.** Having age–appropriate curfews is a necessary part of providing protection.

♦ Why do you think this is the case? _____

_____

♦ How does this rule protect you? _____

_____

♦ What freedoms or benefits does this rule give you? _____

_____

◆ Write out your Freedom Rule that relates to the idea of when to be home. _____

_____

❖ **Freedom Rule #5 – Avoid Alcohol and Drugs.** Besides the damage that alcohol can do to developing minds and bodies, the consumption of alcohol by minors is illegal in every state in the Union. Drugs are also illegal in every state.

◆ How does this rule protect you? _____

_____

◆ What freedoms or benefits does this rule give you? _____

_____

◆ Write out your Freedom Rule that relates to the idea of avoiding alcohol and drugs. _____

_____

❖ **Freedom Rule #6 – Avoid "At-Risk" Situations.** This rule reminds you to stay away from situations that could turn into risky situations, such as parties and get-togethers where alcohol or drugs are being used or where sexual activity is taking place.

◆ How does this rule protect you? _____

_____

◆ What freedoms or benefits does this rule give you? _____

_____

◆ Write out your Freedom Rule that relates to the idea of avoiding risky situations. _____

_____

❖ **Freedom Rule #7 – Watch What You Watch.** This rule helps you learn how to be selective about what you see on TV, in the movies, and in magazines. This includes, but is not limited to, pornography, violence (especially sexual violence), and subtle sexual messages.

◆ How does this rule protect you? _____

_____

◆ What freedoms or benefits does this rule give you? _____

_____

◆ Write out your Freedom Rule that relates to the idea of learning how to decide what to watch. _____

_____

❖ **Freedom Rule #8 – Screen the 'Net.** This is similar to Freedom Rule #7. It helps you learn to be selective about what you do on the Internet.

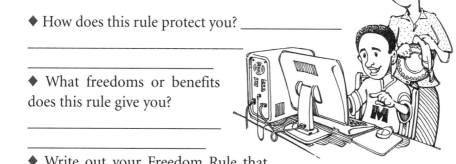

◆ How does this rule protect you? _____

_____

◆ What freedoms or benefits does this rule give you?

_____

◆ Write out your Freedom Rule that relates to the idea of learning how to decide what to see and do on the Internet. _____

_____

❖ **Freedom Rule #9 – Tame the Tunes.** This rule helps you learn how choose the music you listen to. It is similar to the two previous rules.

◆ How does this rule protect you? _____

_____

◆ What freedoms or benefits does this rule give you? _____

_____

◆ Write out your Freedom Rule that relates to the idea of learning how to select the music you listen to. _____

_____

❖ **Freedom Rule #10 – Set Personal Boundaries.** This is a very important boundary that only you can set. If you learn to set your own healthy, personal boundaries in your life, you will be protecting yourself and your future. A specific personal boundary relates to how far you will go sexually.

◆ How does this rule protect you? _____

_____

◆ What freedoms or benefits does this rule give you? _____

_____

◆ Write out your Freedom Rule that relates to the idea of where to set a personal boundary. _____

_____

Look at the following chart and mark where you have set your personal boundary.

SEXUAL PROGRESSION

Holding hands

Hugging

Kissing

Deep kissing

Bodily caressing

Outercourse

Oral sex

Intercourse

Write out your Freedom Rule that relates to the idea of where to set a personal boundary. _____

_____

9

Step Nine

Teach Refusal Skills

Learning How to Say "NO"

In Step One, we looked at the five influences that push teens towards sexual activity – hormones, sex in the media, peers, alcohol, and relationships. Two of the strongest sources of pressure come from peers. Much of this pressure comes from friends who are either sexually active, or who say they are. Relationship pressure applied by that "special someone" creates the other point of intense stress.

Why are teens so vulnerable to peer pressure? Because one of the things teens fear most is rejection by their friends. They need to be accepted by peers, especially in the early teen years when they are so unsure of themselves. Challenged with new experiences, strange feelings, and rapidly developing bodies, young teens feel like others are judging them all the time. Older teens are more comfortable with their bodies; typically they have learned to adjust to the changes. While they still seek peer approval, they are capable of less dependence on one group or one person for total acceptance. Both older and younger teens, however, will look for another crowd to accept them if they feel rejected by a preferred crowd. Unfortunately, the group that accepts them may not be the best crowd for shaping their values and actions.

Just Say No! Easier Said Than Done!

This need for acceptance creates problems for teens who desire abstinence, yet struggle with the pressure applied by friends and that special someone. The following teens faced the pressure and gave in. Their sad words spell out their personal disappointment in themselves.

"When I was pressured, I wasn't able to say 'NO' – I did more than I felt comfortable with." [1]

"I gave in and did it – I couldn't say no." [2]

"When I lost my virginity I was pressured into it. I didn't even know what was going on . . . I was so naive." [3]

"The first time I had sex was because of peer pressure – it was guys saying 'You gotta have sex . . . If you don't, you're not a man.'" [4]

"Like, I get more pressure from my friends than I do from the actual guy. Like, all my friends are like, 'Do it! Do it!' It feels like I'll be cool if I do it." [5]

These teens are not alone. Just saying "NO" can be tough. In a study done by the Kaiser Family Foundation, "Eighty-six percent of teens say young people today face pressure when it comes to sex and relationships."[6] In the same study, teens revealed that two of the top five major reasons for having sex involved pressure from others – the other person wanted to (45 percent) and many of their friends already had (16 percent).[7] Almost half of all teens – 47 percent – said they felt pressured by friends to participate in a sexual act even though they didn't feel ready. Teenage girls are more likely to feel this kind of pressure than teenage boys.[8] Surprisingly, most teens feel like they are less experienced than their friends.

When asked what leads to first-time sexual encounters, more than half the teen girls said it was because they believed they were in love. Guys said their first experience occurred because they had the opportunity and took it.[9] The younger the teen, the less likely the sex was voluntary. Seven out of ten girls who had sex before the age of 13 reported that the sex was involuntary or unwanted.[10]

How Would Your Teen Handle the Pressure?

Most parents want to believe that they have given their children the skills and the resources to handle life on a day-to-day basis. Remembering that you no longer can control your child's environment, how well would your teen do in the following situations?

- Firmly tell a girlfriend or boyfriend "NO" when asked to have sex.
- Be able to explain personal reasons for not having sex, even when pushed by a girlfriend or boyfriend.
- Stick with a previous decision to remain abstinent until marriage.
- Stop seeing a boyfriend or girlfriend, if the passion is getting too hot to handle.
- Walk away from a relationship in which the other person doesn't respect your teen's stand against sex before marriage.
- Refuse to let others influence him or her into having sex because "Everyone's doing it."
- Take the teasing of others about being a virgin.
- Choose a new set of friends, if sex becomes a major focus of the current relationships.

These are typical, peer pressure situations that every teen faces. Unless your teen stays home most of the time, he or she will be confronted with similar situations. Sometimes the situation is serious, and the teen may be struggling to find balance between a friendship and a pledge. Other times, the situation may be a spur-of-the-moment event, where sex is available in a casual situation, such as a party or hanging out with friends with time on their hands and nothing to do. Other factors related to peer pressure involve teens who are curious, drinking, or trying to keep up with the others; these teens may have sex just for the fun of it.

Because these situations occur, teens need to learn basic refusal skills – how to say "NO" when pressured to do something they don't want to do. One third of those in the Kaiser study said they would like to know more about how to talk to a boyfriend or girlfriend about what they feel comfortable doing sexually.[11]

What Do The Experts Do?

Here's how our abstinent teens in the survey responded to the question, "How did you handle the pressure to go farther, or to do something sexual that you didn't want to do?"

"I told him I was not going to have sex – and explained why."

"I took myself out of the situation and physically left."

"I tried talking to my girlfriend about it . . . but she kept coming on. So I dumped her."

"I told him straight up I was feeling pressured and would not have sex with him, and if he didn't like it he could find someone else."

Peer Proofing Your Teen – Set It! Say It! Show It!

Thousands of teens across the country have been tremendously responsive to the following three-step process of "peer proofing" introduced in our *Choosing the Best* curriculum. You can help your teenager apply the same process.

Peer Proofing Step 1 – Set It!

Before teens get caught up in the hormone surges and the powerful passions of the "heat of the moment," they need to evaluate their own convictions and set their personal boundaries. Here's how one teenage girl explained her misjudgment of the high level of emotions:

"I fully understand now, when I got physically involved with somebody, what the 'heat of the moment' means, because it's a whole different ball game when you're actually there." [12]

Previous steps in this book have prepared the way for your teen to use these peer-proofing steps. First, in Step Four you shared with your teen the basics of the abstinence pledge. This is the foundation upon which everything else builds. Next, Step Eight provided an opportunity to set clearly defined boundaries with your teen. Setting limits gives your teen confidence. These comments from several teens explain the importance of setting boundaries.

"If you set clear limits and you can stick to them, you won't have to worry about going too far or getting someone to like you . . . you'll be in charge." [13]

"The most important thing for me is taking charge of who I am, and knowing who I am, and not obsessing over what one guy may think of me, even if I like him." [14]

"There is going to be a little boundary, and then there's going to be a greater boundary; something I'm definitely not going to go over." [15]

Remember, to be most effective, your teen must set his or her own personal boundaries. You can set rules that provide some boundaries for your teen. But, in some areas you can only suggest other boundaries for your son or daughter to consider. Once your teen buys into your suggested boundary – internalizes it – the teen is more willing to stick with it.

Peer Proofing Step 2 – Say It!

It's one thing to set personal boundaries, but teens must also speak up. Consider how tough this is for teens who already fear rejection. Speaking up may result in instant ridicule. Saying what a teen believes could cause a relationship to end. Do you remember how hard it was to express your thoughts when you were a teen? Some teens lack communication skills; they struggle with putting thoughts into words. That's another reason that it's important to work on these skills ahead of time.

Consider the following examples of common situations teens face, in which they experience pressure from their peers to be sexually active.

The Guys

On Darin's basketball team, the guys constantly talk about girls and sex. Darin has dated Angel for the past six months and spends a lot of time with her. They have decided to be abstinent. After one practice, the guys really harass Darin about Angel and their commitment to abstinence. These are Darin's good buddies, so he doesn't want to lose the friendships, but what can he say to them about his commitment?

The Girls

Paula is spending the night with two other girls on her soccer team, Kendra and Leslie. As the evening progresses, talk turns to guys. Both Kendra and Leslie are sexually active with their boyfriends, and they talk about how much fun sex is. Both girls want to know why Paula hasn't done it yet with her boyfriend, Jesse. Paula tries to tell them why she chooses to be abstinent, but Kendra and Leslie insist she could protect herself with birth control pills and a condom and still enjoy a great relationship with Jesse. Paula struggles with the pressure from her friends.

Here's How to Respond

Let's look at four verbal skills that can help your teen master the art of saying "NO."

• **Putdown/Comeback** – When friends apply pressure with a **putdown**, the teen can offer a **comeback**. Here's an example of a putdown/comeback:

> **Putdown** *"Aren't you tired of being a virgin?"*
> **Comeback** *"No, I'm not tired of being free from STDs or a baby or the emotional stress of a sexual relationship. I'm looking forward to the action with my wife/husband when I get married."*

• **Line/Linebacker** – When a teen hears a **line** from a date, the teen can use a **linebacker**. All of us have been in this situation. Can you remember some of the lines you heard when you were dating? Would you admit to using a few lines yourself, just to get a date? In the *Choosing the Best* books, teens have a chance to match up responses to several common lines. Here are a few examples:

> **Line** *"Come on. Everybody's doing it!"*
> **Linebacker** *"Then you won't have trouble finding someone else."*

> **Line** *"If you really love me, then prove it!"*
> **Linebacker** *"If you love me, you'll respect my feelings and stop pushing."*

> **Line** *"You owe me something."*
> **Linebacker** *"I didn't know you put a price on our friendship. If so, I'm canceling this I.O.U. now."*

When you are working through the Discussion section, ask your teen to share several lines he or she has heard. Share a couple of your favorites, too.

• **"YES-NO-YES"** – When a teen wants to maintain the relationship, but must say "NO," he or she can say **"YES-NO-YES."** Sounds a little indecisive, but it's actually a persuasive idea. In **"YES-NO-YES,"** the teen sends three messages: one is positive **YES**, the second is negative **NO**, but the final statement is positive **YES**, and offers an alternative. Here's an example of how this skill works:

> 1.) Your teen's special friend remarks, *"No one's at my house all day. Why don't you come home with me and let's see what happens?"*

> 2.) Your teen responds, first with a positive statement – the **YES**, *"You know I like being with you."*

> 3.) The next response is a negative statement – the **NO**, *"But I'm not sure it's a good idea for us to be alone like that."*

4.) The third response, an alternative idea, is the positive statement that keeps the friendship going – the **YES**, *"Let's grab a pizza, then go rollerblading in the park."*

• **Defense/Offense** – The final "Say It!" skill is to move from the **defense** to the **offense.** Sometimes a date applies pressure by putting the other person on the defensive. The best response is for your teen to grab the offense and express his or her feelings about being pressured constantly. These two phrases can help get the offense rolling: *"When you do . . . I feel . . ."* or *"When you say . . . I feel . . ."* Here's an example:

> *"When you keep pressuring me to have sex with you, after I say no, I feel like you don't really care about me."*

Peer Proofing Step 3 – Show It!

Once your teen has set those sexual boundaries, he or she can learn to speak up to defend those boundaries. Another way to impact peer pressure in a positive way is to show it through body language. To help a teenager remember the five ways to use body language to be assertive, *Choosing the Best* materials provide a visual aid of a body outline (see the Discussion section). Let me briefly explain the five ways to be assertive, and then you can share them with your teen.

1.) The **head** is the place decisions are made about a person's standards, boundaries, and goals. Being assertive begins with a decision that has been thought out. That's why we spent time giving you information to help your teen decide where to draw the boundaries and what goals to establish.

2.) The **heart** is the symbolic place of emotions and character. Being assertive about a desire to remain abstinent grows from a genuine desire to care for, respect, and value both themselves and others.

Remember Dr. Freda Bush's story in Step Three? She and her husband didn't really get the abstinence-until-marriage speech nailed down until they added the character part. Character counts. The character traits of respect for self and others, courage to take a stand, determination to stick with a commitment, and compassion all strengthen a teen's ability to be assertive.

3.) The **mouth** is the body part that says "NO" in a firm, strong manner. Humor can be useful; remember some of the linebackers? Giving reasons (taking the offense) and offering alternatives ("YES-NO-YES") are different ways teens can respond in sexual situations. One danger here is that some teens say "NO" with their words, but "YES" with their actions or their clothing.

4.) That leads us to **body language**. Being assertive can be reflected in how a teen holds his body, the way she looks to others, and even the way the teen stands or sits. Body language sends out strong signals. Other teens will take advantage of a teen whose shoulders are bowed, whose head is down, and whose demeanor is mousy. Or, a flirtatious teen may say "NO" verbally, but communicate "YES" in every other way.

5.) The final way to be assertive involves the **feet**. Sometimes the most assertive action is to walk away from the pressure. Walking away can be a temporary thing that breaks up the passionate mood or slows down the sexual activity. Or, if the pressure continues, the teen may have to walk away from the friendship for good.

As you talk to your teen while using the Discussion section, consider what you've read in this step. In the discussion, your teen will have a chance to evaluate which tools work best for him or her in real-life situations.

Parent: Let's Think About It!

Rate yourself to see how well you have communicated with your teen about good refusal skills. Use a scale of one to five:

1 It's never occurred to me to do this.

2 I've thought about it.

3 I tried, but got no response from my teen.

4 I've done this once.

5 I do this often.

_____ 1. I talk to my teen about the intense pressure from peers, both friends and dates.

_____ 2. I talk to my teen about how alcohol removes inhibitions and lowers a person's resistance to stick by personal morals and previous commitments.

_____ 3. I talk to my teen about practical ways to handle potentially difficult sexual situations.

_____ 4. I talk to my teen about how to get out of a tight sexual situation.

_____ 5. I talk to my teen about how to set personal boundaries.

_____ 6. I talk to my teen about how to say "NO" without losing the friend.

_____ 7. I talk to my teen about what body language and clothing say about a person.

_____ 8. I talk to my teen about how to be assertive, without being aggressive.

_____ 9. I give my teen support and encouragement to stick with his or her personal commitment to abstinence.

_____ 10. I know my teen's friends and dates, so I can better understand the pressure applied by them.

Add up your score. If you have 45 to 50 points, you are either kidding yourself or you have excellent communication with your teen. If you have 38 to 44 points, you are trying to stay in touch with your teen, but you can improve your efforts! If you have 30 to 37 points, you continue to struggle with talking with your teen. Don't give up; it will be worth the effort! If you have 29 or fewer points, don't give up. Possibly you have learned a few things in this step that you can apply to future discussions with your teen.

Parent and Teen: Let's Talk About It!
Discussion Nine – Learning How to Say "NO"

1. **Feeling the Pressure.** According to a recent survey, 86 percent of today's teens say they feel pressured about sex and relationships. Read the following comments from real-life teens like yourself. Then, discuss the questions with your parent.

Girl: *"When I was pressured, I wasn't able to say "NO" – I did more than I felt comfortable with."* [1]

Girl: *"When I lost my virginity I was pressured into it. I didn't even know what was going on . . . I was so naive."* [2]

Guy: *"The first time I had sex was because of peer pressure – it was guys saying 'You gotta have sex . . . If you don't you're not a man.'"* [3]

Girl: *"Like I get more pressure from my friends, than I do from the actual guy. Like, all my friends are like, 'Do it! Do it.'"* [4]

◆ Why would a young person do something that person really didn't want to?

◆ How do you say "NO" to pressure from your friends and still maintain the friendships?

2. **Refusing the Pressure.** How good are your refusal skills? How well do you handle the pressure from others? Rate yourself on how well you handle the following refusal situations:

◆ I can firmly tell a girlfriend or boyfriend "NO" when asked to have sex.

Never   Some of the time   Most of the time   That's me: all the time

◆ I am able to explain my personal reasons for not having sex, even when pushed by a boyfriend or girlfriend.

Never   Some of the time   Most of the time   That's me: all the time

◆ I can walk away from a relationship where the other person doesn't respect my desire to abstain from sex.

Never   Some of the time   Most of the time   That's me: all the time

◆ I can take the teasing from others about being a virgin or a "renewed virgin."

Never   Some of the time   Most of the time   That's me: all the time

◆ I can stick with my decision to remain abstinent until marriage.

Never   Some of the time   Most of the time   That's me: all the time

3. **Learning How to Say "NO."** Sharpening your refusal skills continues with learning how to say "NO" in a way that is heard. Check out these ideas.

❖ When you hear a "**line**," you can respond with a "**linebacker**."

> **Line:** *"Come on. Everybody's doing it."*
> **Linebacker:** *"Then you won't have trouble finding someone else."*

> **Line:** *"If you really love me, then you'll prove it."*
> **Linebacker:** *"If you love me, you'll respect my feelings and stop pressuring me."*

What's another line that you've heard? _____
_____
What might be a good linebacker? _____
_____

❖ When you have to say "NO" to someone special and want to preserve the relationship, say "YES-NO-YES." Here's how it works:

Your friend asks you to do something that is outside your boundaries: *"No one's at my house. Why don't you come home with me?"*

First, make a **positive statement** – **"YES"**: *"I really like spending time with you."*

Second, make a **negative statement** – **"NO"**: *"But, I can't come to your house because I'm not sure I trust myself being alone with you."*

Third, finish with a **positive alternative** – **"YES"**: *"Let's grab a cola and hang out with the others."*

Try it out. Let's say a friend asks you to go to a party where you know there will be alcohol and sex.

YES: _____

NO: _____

YES: _____

❖ Go from the **defense** to the **offense**. When someone special puts you on the defensive and keeps pressuring you, take the **offense** by stating how his or her behavior makes you feel.

You say: *"Look, when you keep pressuring me to have sex after I told you 'No', I feel like you really don't care about me. Now, back off!"*

What can you do if the pressure continues? _____

_____

4. **Learning how to SHOW "NO"!** How you say what you say makes a difference. Being assertive means you use body language to back up your words. Act out the linebackers, the "YES-NO-YES" statements, and the offense statement in two ways: first, use body language that says "YES" while your words say "NO"; second, use body language that says "NO" while your words also are saying "NO."

153

10

Step Ten

Practice Unconditional LOVE

What to Do When Nothing Else Works

How would you feel if you heard one of these real-life confessions from your teen?

> "I started having sex when I was sixteen. It's hard to say 'no' to sex. Now, it's good to have sex, anytime, anyplace, anywhere." [1]

> "I don't think I'm going to wait because foreplay feels good and I'm guessing if the foreplay feels good, sex probably feels good too." [2]

> "I met him at Taco Bell where we both worked, and I guess we just clicked. I don't believe in sex before marriage, but I did it anyways. Now I'm pregnant." [3]

> "We were convinced that we were going to get married some day – we were so much in love. Before I knew what I had done, I had already given myself away to another person, realizing I was supposed to wait for a special day to do that." [4]

> "I think self-control is something I definitely chose not to exercise. I wanted to have sex, so I did, you know? I wanted to go out and party and drink, so I did." [5]

"After my abortion, that baby's father and I broke up. Within six weeks after my abortion, I was involved in another sexual relationship with a different guy." [6]

"I was drunk and I had sex with this girl – I didn't even know her name." [7]

We all know that parenting is an art, not a science. What if you have the best intentions, do everything right with your teen, even complete all 10 discussions of the BIG TALK, then later discover a situation that leaves you feeling powerless and devastated? What do you do as a parent?

What Doesn't Work

Before evaluating what to do when you hear devastating news from your teen, let's identify three common reactions of parents that do *not* work.

• **The Big Scene** – This usually occurs as a natural, knee-jerk reaction to learning about your teen's negative behavior. This is especially true if your teen's behavior involves being sexually active or some other at-risk behavior that you and your teen previously agreed was wrong. With adrenaline rushing and a flushed face, you launch a barrage of words, questions, and emotions at your teen. Of course, you remind the teen about the discussion you had in which, "I told you not to do this" was the theme. Then, there's the pitiful, "How could you do this to me?" The teen reacts with just as much intensity and emotion, defending the behavior with selfish statements. Voices escalate. Words fly out in anger. Doors are slammed. Nothing is accomplished. The problem is not addressed. A solution is not sought. Relationships have just gone from bad to worse. Both individuals do and say things they later regret.

• **The Big Elephant** – In recovery programs, when there is a drinking problem in the family but no one is willing to talk about it, it's called the "big elephant" in the living room. Instead of acknowledging its presence, everyone tiptoes around the subject. Ignoring the problem doesn't solve the problem. As a result, unsolved problems grow worse. Like the Big Scene, people involved in the Big Elephant do not seek a solution. Relationships may be maintained, but they are tenuous and superficial at best.

• **The Big Enabler** – This parental action outwardly appears to be the most noble. To help the troubled teen, the parent cleans up the mess. For example, if the teen becomes pregnant and produces a child, the enabler parent takes over the responsibilities of raising that child. Actually, by not allowing the teen to suffer some of the natural consequences, things grow worse in the long run for the teen. A teen will continue detrimental behavior as long as the enabler parent supplies the resources and handles the consequences. The teen with this type of parent has no incentive to discontinue negative behavior and initiate responsible behavior.

Consequences and Compassion

The key to parenting through a disappointment is to **separate the performance from the person**. Clearly, parents have a right to be upset about the performance of their teens, especially when those teens choose to be involved in at-risk behaviors. At the same time, the teen needs to know that the parents remain committed to the teen's welfare, that the parents still love the teen as a person, and that the parents want what is best for the teenager. To pull this off, parents need to allow most consequences for wrong behavior to occur. At the same time, parents must continue to show as much compassion as possible.

To see one example of how this works, let's consider the real-life case of Melody. In middle school, Melody was the ideal student. She was popular in school, had several close friends, and generally obeyed her parents by coming in by curfew and telling her parents where she was going and with whom.

Her parents had talked to Melody about their expectations for her to be sexually abstinent until marriage. In her last year in middle school, Melody completed an abstinence-focused, sex-education course, which encouraged her and other teens to choose abstinence. No bumps in the road so far . . . until high school.

In middle school, Melody was at the top of her class and knew everyone. In high school, she got lost in the large number of students. Suddenly nobody knew who Melody was – and, even worse, she believed nobody cared. The shaky transition from middle school to high school left her feeling uncertain of herself. Desperately desiring acceptance, she responded to the friendship of "new friends" who had different values. Some of these girls hung out with older guys.

During this time, she pulled away from her parents, saying that it was time she grew up a little. She isolated herself from her old friends, believing they just weren't mature. When her mom tried to talk with her, Melody grew sullen and non-responsive. Her home life felt like a battle zone, as her personal life spiraled out of control. One of the older guys from the group started paying attention to Melody, which helped her sagging self-esteem. But his attention quickly turned to physical demands, which Melody didn't know how to handle.

Like many teens, after that first sexual encounter, Melody experienced a tremendous loss of self-respect. It was compounded when her older boyfriend dropped her several months after they began having sex and started going out with another of Melody's friends. Believing that other guys knew what she had done, she gave herself to one guy after another. On the outside, she pretended it was not a big deal. Yet, inside it was a BIG DEAL.

> *"When I lost my virginity, I was pressured into it. I didn't even know what was going on. Like I said, I was so naive. But after that, it may have been an insecurity of my own that I felt – well, he knows that I had sex with another guy, so he's going to expect it from me, too."*

Melody started coming in after her curfew and seemed to welcome the resulting grounding. Her grades plummeted. Her old friends no longer made any attempt to stay in touch with Melody. Her parents knew something was going on, but attempts to find out were futile. During this time, however, her mother came into her room every night and kissed Melody goodnight. She repeatedly told Melody that she loved her and cared about her, no matter what.

Melody continued her at-risk lifestyle into her sophomore year. Her mom and dad continued to affirm her and love her. And, they continued to hold her accountable for her actions. Mainly, they just hung in there.

Finally, something happened. The natural consequences of the negative emotions from losing her self-respect, experiencing failed relationships, dealing with poor grades, losing her friends, plus facing the fears of pregnancy and STDs caused Melody to hit a brick wall. She realized she no longer wanted to live that way. In her junior year, Melody made the decision on her own to commit to "renewed virginity." With this commitment, Melody decided from that day forward to abstain from sex until marriage. Here's what she says about that decision:

"When I decided to become abstinent, and I stuck to that decision, people seemed to respect me a lot. I just got my report card. I got a 3.5. I'm really proud of that. I was able to focus more on grades and things that mattered in what I wanted to pursue, which is I want to become an elementary school teacher eventually. In October, I made Homecoming Court. That blew me away. It just showed that when you change and learn to respect yourself, others will respect you, too."

"My mom and I have been pretty honest with each other. Our relationship has become better. It's become more open and more honest. It's not like we're trying to hide something. I like having a relationship with my mom where I can talk to her about things." [8]

Unfortunately, I can't promise that every sexually active teen will change like Melody did. Too often, the results of sexual activity are much more severe than those Melody experienced. A teen might end up being a single parent responsible for a baby. The baby might have AIDS or be addicted to drugs or have fetal alcohol syndrome. A teen mother might bear the emotional scars from an abortion or an adoption. The teen might experience the consequences of an incurable, or permanently damaging, STD, or contract a life-threatening disease. But, unconditional love offers compassion and support through the consequences.

> **Renewed Virginity**
> Renewed virginity is the decision to stop having sex. It gives a teenager who has been sexually active a fresh start. While the teen cannot undo the consequences of sexual activity, renewed virginity allows the teen to start over "from this day forward." Many teens choose renewed virginity, because it allows them to protect their emotions, their minds, and their bodies. A CDC report found that among ninth- to 12th-graders who had been sexually active, 27 percent say they are now abstinent.[9]

Melody's story identifies three principles of how to put unconditional love into practice.

Principle 1 – Keep the Relationship Door Open

First, did you notice the consistent reaching out from Melody's mom? She sent a continual message that the relationship with her daughter was important. She expressed her commitment to this relationship in tangible ways, such as the nightly ritual of tucking Melody in and the continued hugs. Even when Melody pulled back, her mom never did.

Is it hard to keep reaching out when you are rejected by your teen and the teen's behavior?

Sure it is! Too often in my years of parenting teens, I would find my relationship with my son Brannon or my daughter Natalie affected by his or her performance. If they did well, I showered them with acceptance. However, when they didn't follow the rules, I pulled back emotionally from the relationship. Fortunately, this is where my wife Donna helped hold relationships together. She would keep the relationship door open even when rules were broken. In Brannon's junior year in high school, he tried to figure out how many rules he could break without getting caught. I took his behavior as a direct challenge and pulled away emotionally. Yet during this time, Donna continued to find ways to connect and send the caring messages that he needed to hear.

If you struggle with being caring and compassionate for the teen who fights against your authority, values, and rules, let me suggest two actions that helped me.

Get Alone and Remember
Pull back from the intensity and emotions of the conflict and be alone. This gives you time to gain perspective. In this time alone, remember that love is not based on what a person does, but on who a person is. Love is a commitment to the well-being of the other person. Reaffirm your parental commitment to the well-being of your teen. Also, recognize that controlling a teen's actions is an illusion. The approach used in childhood of obtaining obedience through rewards and punishments no longer works. You are no longer capable of setting your teen's behavior. To become healthy adults, your teen must separate from you and become responsible for his or her own behavior. While you are alone, write down affirmations of your love and commitment to your teen. State your desire to help your teen move from childhood to adulthood, even if that means the teen becomes someone different from whom you wish him or her to be. While you cannot control your teen, you can influence him or her by your commitment to his or her well-being.

Plan a Time of Affirmation
My second suggested action is to plan a special time of affirmation for your teen. Temporarily take off your parenting hat and put on your

friend hat. Select something your teen enjoys doing, then do it together. My son enjoyed two things we could do together – eating out and sports events. Through our toughest struggles in high school, I still could get a glimmer of response in his eyes when we would go out to eat or when we would go to a sporting event together. The key to this time together was that I would leave my parenting agenda at home. I found that if I was intentional about making the event a time to relate, I could relax and enjoy our time together. When we returned home, of course, I put back on the parenting hat.

Principle 2 – Consequences as Teachers

What are natural consequences? These are the expected results of the actions and choices we make. In the adult world ruled by

natural consequences, if you drive too fast and get caught, you get a ticket. If you over-spend, you end up in debt. If you eat the wrong kinds of food, the result is high cholesterol. If you fail to exercise, you can develop chronic health problems. If you isolate yourself, you lose friends. If you consistently perform poorly on the job, you will be fired.

Learning to accept the consequences of our actions starts early in life, and parents often condition children when they're very young *not* to live with consequences. Remember those all-night sessions when your grade-school child suddenly informed you that her science project was due the next day? Your intentions were admirable; you didn't want her to fail. But the result sent a different message. The child learned, "I can wait until the last minute, and mom and dad will bail me out." Obviously, when this "bailing out" was done infrequently, as an exception, the message was not so strong. But, if every time your child was late on a report or an assignment, you dropped whatever you were doing to help out, what message was becoming hardwired into the brain of your child? Of course! "There is no real consequence for lack of effort and planning." Most parents don't want to teach their children this, because in the real world, procrastinators eventually experience disastrous consequences.

What have you had to do to change poor behavior patterns in your life? Quite often, it is after we experience the negative, natural consequences that the motivation to change kicks in, and we alter our destructive behavior. When creditors make those annoying collection calls, we work out a repayment plan. When forced to pay outrageous fines for speeding, we slow down. When the doctor informs us that our cholesterol is much too high, we change our eating habits.

Too often, well-intentioned parents step in to protect their teens from the natural consequences of their behavior. Parents try to soften the blow, preventing the teen from benefiting from the teachable moment of natural consequences.

So, how does the concept of experiencing natural consequences relate to at-risk sexual behavior? Melody's mom must have known that Melody was unhappy in the lifestyle she had chosen. She probably hoped that Melody eventually would wake up and see the negative consequences of her choices. Her mom was right. Those negative consequences of teen sex that you saw in Step Two began to affect Melody. You saw how sexual activity produces negative emotional consequences and lowers self-esteem. How did this happen in Melody's case?

First, she sought acceptance and love by giving herself sexually. The more she gave physically, the worse she felt emotionally. Melody's parents had to stand by and let her experience those feelings. Second, Melody feared getting pregnant. Fortunately, she did not get pregnant, but the pregnancy factor motivated her to turn her away from her sexual activity. Again, her mother did not try to eliminate the teaching effect of the fear of disease or pregnancy by suggesting that Melody use condoms for "safe sex." Remember that in Step Three, we saw that "safe sex" is really a myth.

What if Melody had not been moved by the natural consequences of her behavior? What if she had continued even farther in her at-risk behaviors? In the following explanations several young people look back on their experiences as teens and share the consequences of their continued sexual behavior. You read some of their stories in Steps Five and Six.

> **Danna:** *"Therapy has helped me more than I can say. I need to just deal with the feelings, and I need to get rid of some of the stuff that was in my past. Because without talking about it, it just got deeper and deeper inside. When I date a guy now, I don't have sex with him, and in a relationship, it takes me a long time to trust. It took a long time to change any of it, and I'm still changing a lot, but it took a very long time to change any of it."* [10]

> **Lathia:** *"Having sex can ruin you physically and mentally. Sex will ruin your relationships in the future. I'm still working on overcoming the negative effects in my life."* [11]

> **Ezra:** *"Sex made me feel really close to the person, and then once it goes away, there is a huge let-down. I should have spent more time on my schoolwork and extracurricular activities, but I was wrapped up in my relationship. Now, I've learned that sex actually hurts a relationship. When I get involved in a relationship [now], we develop a strong foundation without sex."* [12]

What happened in the lives of these young people? A lot of learning took place. They learned about the need to build healthy relationships, and about how unhealthy relationships harm a person. They learned about developing as a person with self-respect. In each case, the learning came as the result of natural consequences.

Here's a tough one. What if the consequences involve a teen pregnancy and a child to care for? Michelle tells her story:

> *"Right now for me to cover the bills and expenses I have, I have to work a lot of hours. This wasn't my mom's baby, so I felt like I had to make it work myself. Because I wasn't able to complete my education, I*

cannot obtain the kind of job that would give my son the things he so rightfully deserves. To want a family is important. But this is not the way to go about doing it. There is a better way to do it that will cause you less pain. I thought I was going to be Betty Crocker. I was going to be the perfect mother, but I'm still struggling." [13]

These natural consequences are painful. Any parent wants to shield their daughter or son from these situations. But, the learning that comes from the experiences of natural consequences produces insightful, adult-oriented thinking and character. So, what do we parents do while waiting on the consequences to do the teaching? That's the third principle of unconditional love.

Principle 3 – Keep the Light On!

You never know when the turning point will occur, so keep the light on. Stay hopeful. Expect that something will bring a change. In the meantime, be proactive. Stay available. Be persistent in your care and the compassion you show your teen.

This does not mean that you waver in your values. By offering love and compassion, you are not embracing your teen's values. Instead, continue to communicate your commitment to your teen as a person of worth. How is this done?

Think Long-Term

Think long-term, not just next week. Parents often fall into the trap of wanting things to change overnight. Then, when expectations fail to be met quickly, the parent backs away from a relationship with the teen. Sorry! Real life doesn't happen that way.

Teen Under Construction

Keep this mental sign over your teen, "Under Construction." That means a lot of learning still needs to take place. By visualizing that sign you will remember to step back and give the teen a chance to learn from the instructor of natural consequences.

Parent Under Construction

Ask yourself, what do you need to be learning? We parents remain under construction, too. Parenting is one of the most difficult assignments in life, and no one is born knowing how. Talk about on-the-job-training! Continue to learn about yourself and how to communicate love and acceptance. View this time with your teenager as an opportunity for you to learn and develop too.

Keep On Keeping On

Keep on loving. True love for your child doesn't waver despite how the teen treats you. (That's performance love – "If you do this specific behavior, then I will love and accept you."). Teens notice how parents react when they throw everything negative at them. By their very actions, teens are asking, "Do you really love me?" Your constant answer has to be, "You are my child, and I will always love you. There is nothing you can do to make me love you more. And, nothing you do can make me love you less. I love you period."

With unconditional love you win. And they win.

Parent: Let's Think About It!

1. What's the most devastating news you've had from your teenager?

   • How did you handle it?

   • If you had it to do over again, what would you change? Why? How?

   • What change has come from the situation?

2. How do you most often react to difficult situations with your teen? (Check only one.)
   ❏ The Big Scene
   ❏ The Big Elephant
   ❏ The Big Enabler
   ❏ The Great Compassion Giver
   ❏ The Natural Consequences

3. What's the toughest thing about being a parent of a teenager?

4. What suggestions from Step 10 can help you in your parenting?

5. If you could talk back to the author of this book, which of these sentences would you use for your discussion? Why?

   _____ The key to parenting through a disappointment is to separate the performance from the person.

   _____ Love is a commitment to the well-being of the other person.

   _____ Temporarily take off your parenting hat and put on your friend hat.

   _____ The learning that comes from the experiences of natural consequences produces insightful, adult-oriented thinking and character.

   _____ Expect that something will bring a change.

   _____ True love for your child doesn't waver despite how the teen treats you.

Parent and Teen: Let's Talk About It!
Discussion Ten – Keeping the Communication Lines Open

1. **What If?** Read the following stories from real-life teens. Then, discuss the questions with your parent.

> **Girl**: *"I think self-control is something I definitely chose not to exercise. I wanted to have sex, so I did. I wanted to go out and party and drink, so I did."* [1]

♦ What advice would you give to the parent of this teen?

♦ What advice would you give to the girl?

> **Guy**: *"I was drunk and had sex with this girl – I didn't even know her name."* [2]

♦ What advice would you give to the parent of this teen?

♦ What advice would you give to the guy?

2. **The Wrong Way to Respond.** Discuss the shortcomings of each of the three ways parents and teens typically respond to disagreements.

❖ The BIG SCENE. This usually occurs when a parent learns about a teen's negative behavior, especially if it involves a behavior that the parent and teen have talked about as unacceptable. Tempers grow hot. Words fly. Doors slam.

♦ How does a teen feel when this happens?

♦ How does a parent feel when this happens?

♦ How can we avoid the BIG SCENE?

169

❖ The BIG ELEPHANT. In this situation, everyone knows there is a problem – like a big elephant in the living room – but no one talks about it. Neither the parent nor the teen acknowledges the situation.

◆ How does a teen feel when this happens?

◆ How does a parent feel when this happens?

◆ How can we avoid the BIG ELEPHANT?

❖ The BIG ENABLER. This happens when the parent tries to rescue or protect the teen without letting the teen experience any natural consequences. For example, if the teen becomes pregnant, the parents accept the cost and responsibility for raising their daughter's child.

◆ How does a teen feel when this happens?

◆ How does a parent feel when this happens?

◆ How can we avoid the BIG ENABLER?

3. **A Better Way – Natural Consequences.** When bad decisions are made, the consequences of those decisions serve as teachers to help us in the future. Experiencing natural consequences reminds us to avoid a certain behavior the next time. For example, in the adult world, if we drive too fast and get caught, we get a ticket.

◆ What are some other natural consequences adults might encounter from poor choices or behaviors? _____

_____

◆ What are some natural consequences the two teens in the examples above might experience?

Girl: _____

Guy: _____

◆ **Teen:** Share a time when natural consequences taught you a lesson that you won't forget. _____

_____

◆ **Parent:** Share a time when natural consequences taught you a lesson that you won't forget._____

_____

4. **Now, What?** For the last few weeks you have had a planned time of specific communication.

◆ What are some ways to keep communication lines open in the future? _____

◆ **Teen:** What has been most helpful to you in working through these 10 sessions? _____

◆ **Parent:** What has been most helpful to you in working through these 10 sessions? _____

Notes

Notes

Notes

Notes

Notes

Notes

Endnotes

Introduction: You Are More Important Than You Think!

1. Kaiser Family Foundation and *seventeen* magazine, "National Survey of Teens About Sex: Decision Making," September 2000.

2. Ibid.

3. Center for Parent/Youth Understanding, "Youth Culture – Family," *Culture Fast Facts* March 15, 2002 http://www.cpyu.org/culture.hmt.

4. Center for Parent/Youth Understanding, "Youth Culture – School," *Culture Fast Facts* March 15, 2002

5. National Crime Prevention Council. "Are We Safe? Major Finding: Many Influences in Decisions About Right and Wrong," Th*e 2001 National Crime Prevention Survey.*

6. National Campaign to Prevent Teen Pregnancy. (2003). With One Voice 2003: America's adults and teens sound off about teen pregnancy. Washington D.C: Author.

7. National Campaign To Prevent Teen Pregnancy: With One Voice 2004, "America's Adults and Teens Sound Off About Teen Pregnancy", December 2004.

8. Northwestern University Medical School: Mental Health Services and Evaluation Program. "Abstinence Focused Sex Education Curriculum Research Study." 1994-1995.

Step One: Be Informed

1. Centers for Disease Control and Prevention, "Youth Risk Behavior Surveillance – United States," 2003.

2. The Alan Guttmacher Institute, Sex and America's Teenagers, New York, AGI, 1994. Calculated by AGI on the basis of data from the Centers for Disease Control and Prevention, Division of HIV/STD prevention, 1992 Annual Report, Atlanta, 1993; Forrest and Singh, 1990; Harlap, Kost, and Forrest, 1991; Sonenstein, Pleck and Ku, 1989; U.S. Bureau of the Census, 1990.

3. Alan Guttmacher Institute, Teenage pregnancy: overall trends and state-by-state information, New York: AGI, 1999, Table 1; and Henshaw SK, U.S. Teenage pregnancy statistics with comparative statistics for women aged 20- 24, New York: AGI, 1999, p. 5.

4. Paul Robertson, "Making the Young Old Before Their Time," *CPYU Newsletter Archives*, quoting Joan Jacob Bromberg in her book, *The Body Project.*

5. "Understanding Puberty," *KidsHealth*, February 2001.

6. Center for Parent/Youth Understanding, "Delaying Marriage," *Culture Fast Facts*, March 15, 2002.

7. United States House of Representatives, *Marketing Violent Entertainment to Children: Self-*

Regulation and Industry Practices in the Motion Picture, Music Recording, and Electronic Game Industries before the Subcommittee on Telecommunications and the Internet, Committee on Energy and Commerce, Washington, D. C., July 20, 2001.

8. National Institute on Media and the Family. *KidScore.*

9. Ibid.

10. Ibid.

11. Preview Online. http://www.gospelcom.net/preview/freerev.php3?2013.

12. Kaiser Family Foundation, "More TV Shows Include Sexual Content; Safer Sex Messages Most Common When Teen Characters or Sexual Intercourse Are Involved," February 6, 2001.

13. Kaiser Family Foundation, "Teens Say Sex on TV Influences Behavior of Peers: Some Positive Effects Seen" May 20, 2002.

14. Kaiser Family Foundation, "Sex on TV: Executive Summary." A Biennial Report to the Kaiser Family Foundation, 1999.

15. Kaiser, "More TV Shows."

16. "Keri Russell and the Felicity Factor," *seventeen* magazine, April 2002; interview segment.

17. Steven Isaac, "Dawson's Creek" *Plugged In*, March 2001.

18. National Institute on Media and the Family, "MTV," *FactSheets.*

19. Ibid.

20. John King, "Federal report finds entertainment industry aims marketing at children," CNN.com *U.S. News*, September 11, 2000.

21. U.S. House, *Marketing Violence.*

22. Center for Parent/Youth Understanding, "Youth Culture – Technology," *Culture Fast Facts*, March 15, 2002; and Kaiser Family Foundation, "New Study Finds Kids Spend Equivalent of Full Work Week Using Media," November 17, 1999.

23. The National Council on Sexual Addiction and Compulsivity, "Cybersex and Sexual Addiction," 2000.

24. Kaiser / *seventeen*, "Decision Making."

25. Kaiser Family Foundation and *YM* magazine, "National Survey of Teens on Dating, Intimacy, and Sexual Experiences," Spring 1998.

26. The National Center on Addiction and Substance Abuse at Columbia University (CASA). Dangerous Liasons, December 7, 1999.

27. Ibid.

28. Jeanie Fleming, "Young, Eager, and Drunk," *WebMD Medical News*, May 15, 2000.

29. Cohen, L.L., & Shotland, R.L. (1996). Timing of first sexual intercourse in a relationship: Expectations, experiences, and perceptions of others. The Journal of Sex Research, 33, 291-299.

30. Kaiser / *seventeen*, "Decision Making."

31. CDC / YRBSS, 2003.

32. Ibid.

33. Kaiser / *YM.*

Discussion One – "Everybody's Talking About It!"

1. CDC/YRBSS, 2003.

2. The Alan Guttmacher Institute, Sex and America's Teenagers, New York, AGI, 1994. Calculated by AGI on the basis of data from the Centers for Disease Control and Prevention, Division of HIV/STD prevention, 1992 Annual Report, Atlanta, 1993; Forrest and Singh, 1990; Harlap, Kost, and Forrest, 1991; Sonenstein, Pleck and Ku, 1989; U.S. Bureau of the Census, 1990.

3. Rector, R.E., Johnson, K.A., Noyes, L.R. Sexually Active Teenagers Are More Likely to Be Depressed and to Attempt Suicide. Heritage Center for Data Analysis Report. CDA03-04, June 2, 2003.

4. KidScore.

5. No Apologies: The Truth About Life, Love & Sex, Focus on the Family. (Video)

6. Real People: Teens Who Choose Abstinence, Sunburst Technology Corp. (Video)

7. Ibid.

8. Weinstock H., Berman S. and Cates W., Jr., Sexually transmitted diseases among American youth; incidence and prevalence estimates, Perspectives on Sexual and Reproductive Health, 2004, 36 (1): 6-10.

9. Alan Guttmacher Institute, Teenage pregnancy: overall trends and state-by-state information, New York: AGI, 1999, Table 1; and Henshaw SK, U.S. Teenage pregnancy statistics with comparative statistics for women aged 20- 24, New York: AGI, 1999, p. 5.]

Step Two: Explain the Risks

1. Centers for Disease Control and Prevention. Tracking the hidden epidemics, 2000: Trends in the United States. Retrieved November 2005 from http://www.cdc.gov/nchstp/od/news/RevBrochure1pdf.htm.

2. Alan Guttmacher Institute, Teenage pregnancy: overall trends and state-by-state information, New York: AGI, 1999, Table 1; and Henshaw SK, U.S. Teenage pregnancy statistics with comparative statistics for women aged 20- 24, New York: AGI, 1999, p. 5.]

3. National Campaign to Prevent Teen Pregnancy (2004). Recent Trends in Teen Pregnancy, Sexual Activity, and Contraceptive Use. Washington, D.C.: 2004.

4. Weinstock H., Berman S. and Cates W., Jr., Sexually transmitted diseases among American youth; incidence and prevalence estimates, Perspectives on Sexual and Reproductive Health, 2004, 36 (1): 6-10.

5. No Apologies. (Video)

6. Ibid.

7. Ibid.

8. Ibid.

9. Ibid.

10. Ibid.

11. Rector et al., "Sexually Active Teenagers Are More Likely to be Depressed and Attempt Suicide," Heritage Foundation, June, 2003.

12. Ibid.

13. National Campaign To Prevent Teen Pregnancy: With One Voice 2004, "America's Adults and Teens Sound Off About Teen Pregnancy", December 2004.

14. National Campaign to Prevent Teen Pregnancy (2004). Recent Trends in Teen Pregnancy, Sexual Activity, and Contraceptive Use. Washington, D.C.: 2004.

15. Alan Guttmacher Institute, Teenage pregnancy: overall trends and state-by-state information, New York: AGI, 1999, Table 1; and Henshaw SK, U.S. Teenage pregnancy statistics with comparative statistics for women aged 20- 24, New York: AGI, 1999, p. 5.]

16. *Teen Files: The Truth About Sex*, AIMS Multimedia. (Video)

17. The Robin Hood Foundation, "Kids Having Kids: A Robin Hood Foundation Special Report on the Costs of Adolescent Childbearing," R. A. Maynard, editor, 1996.

18. Ibid.

19. National Campaign to Prevent Teen Pregnancy. (1997). Whatever Happened to Childhood? The Problem of Teen Pregnancy in the United States. Washington, DC.

20. The Robin Hood Foundation.

21. NCTPTP, "Whatever Happened".

22. *Teen Files.* (Video)

23. Centers for Disease Control and Prevention. Tracking the hidden epidemics, 2000: Trends in the United States. Retrieved November 2005 from http://www.cdc.gov/nchstp/od/news/RevBrochure1pdf.htm.

24. Ibid.

25. Ibid.

26. The Alan Guttmacher Institute, Sex and America's Teenagers, New York, AGI, 1994. Calculated by AGI on the basis of data from the Centers for Disease Control and Prevention, Division of HIV/STD prevention, 1992 Annual Report, Atlanta, 1993; Forrest and Singh, 1990; Harlap, Kost, and Forrest, 1991; Sonenstein, Pleck and Ku, 1989; U.S. Bureau of the Census, 1990.

27. Kaiser / MTV / *Teen People.*

28. Kaiser / *seventeen*, "Sexually Transmitted Diseases."

29. Lisa Remez, "Oral Sex Among Adolescents: Is It Sex or Is It Abstinence?" *Family Planning Perspectives.* Vol. 32, No. 6, November/December 2000, 299.

30. Centers for Disease Control and Prevention. Tracking the hidden epidemics, 2000: Trends in the United States. Retrieved November 2005 from http://www.cdc.gov/nchstp/od/news/RevBrochure1pdf.htm.

31. Weinstock H., Berman S. and Cates W., Jr., Sexually transmitted diseases among American youth; incidence and prevalence estimates, Perspectives on Sexual and Reproductive Health, 2004, 36 (1): 6-10.

32. Centers for Disease Control and Prevention. Tracking the hidden epidemics, 2000: Trends in the United States. Retrieved November 2005 from http://www.cdc.gov/nchstp/od/news/RevBrochure1pdf.htm.

33. The Alan Guttmacher Institute, Sex and America's Teenagers, New York, AGI, 1994.

34. ASHA / Kaiser.

35. Centers for Disease Control and Prevention. Tracking the hidden epidemics, 2000: Trends in the United States. Retrieved November 2005 from http://www.cdc.gov/nchstp/od/news/RevBrochure1pdf.htm.

36. Centers for Disease Control and Prevention. Gonorrhea Fact Sheet. Retrieved November 2005 from http://www.cdc.gov/std/healthcomm/fact_sheets.htm.

37. Centers for Disease Control and Prevention. Tracking the hidden epidemics, 2000: Trends in the United States. Retrieved November 2005 from http://www.cdc.gov/nchstp/od/news/RevBrochure1pdf.htm.

38. Centers for Disease Control and Prevention. Genital HPV Fact Sheet. Retrieved

November 2005 from http://www.cdc.gov/std/healthcomm/fact sheets.htm.

39. Ibid.

40. Centers for Disease Control and Prevention. Tracking the hidden epidemics, 2000: Trends in the United States. Retrieved November 2005 from http://www.cdc.gov/nchstp/od/news/ RevBrochure1pdf.htm.

41. Ibid.

42. Fleming DT, McQuillian GM, Johnson RE, et al. Herpes Simplex Virus Type 2 in the United States, 1976 to 1994. N Engl J Med 1997;337 (16):1105-11.

43. UNAIDS, AIDS Epidemic Update, December, 2004.

44. CDC HIV/AIDS Fact Sheet: CDC HIV/AIDS Surveillance Report, 2003.

45. Ibid.

46. Centers for Disease Control and Prevention, "The role of STD detection and treatment in HIV prevention", retrieved August 2005 from http://www.cdc.gov/std/hiv/STDFact-STD&HIV.htm.

Discussion Two – Understanding the Risks

1. *No Apologies.* (Video)

2. Ibid.

3. Rector, R.E., Johnson, K.A., Noyes, L.R. Sexually Active Teenagers Are More Likely to Be Depressed and to Attempt Suicide. Heritage Center for Data Analysis Report. CDA03-04, June 2, 2003.

4. Ibid.

5. *Teen Files.* (Video)

6. 20/20 ABC News Show, September 3rd, 1999: "*Intimate Dangers*".

7. Ibid.

8. Centers for Disease Control and Prevention. Tracking the hidden epidemics, 2000: Trends in the United States. Retrieved November 2005 from http://www.cdc.gov/nchstp/od/news/ RevBrochure1pdf.htm.

9. Centers for Disease Control and Prevention. Tracking the hidden epidemics, 2000: Trends in the United States. Retrieved November 2005 from http://www.cdc.gov/nchstp/od/news/ RevBrochure1pdf.htm.

10. The Alan Guttmacher Institute, Sex and America's Teenagers, New York, AGI, 1994.

11. 20/20 ABC News Show, "Intimate Dangers," September 3, 1999.

12. Centers for Disease Control and Prevention. Tracking the hidden epidemics, 2000: Trends in the United States. Retrieved November 2005 from http://www.cdc.gov/nchstp/od/news/ RevBrochure1pdf.htm.

13. Centers for Disease Control and Prevention. Genital HPV Fact Sheet. Retrieved November 2005 from http://www.cdc.gov/std/healthcomm/fact sheets.htm.

14. Ibid.

15. 20/20 ABC News Show.

16. Centers for Disease Control and Prevention. Tracking the hidden epidemics, 2000: Trends in the United States. Retrieved November 2005 from http://www.cdc.gov/nchstp/od/news/ RevBrochure1pdf.htm.

17. UNAIDS, AIDS Epidemic Update, December, 2004.

18. CDC HIV/AIDS Fact Sheet: CDC HIV/AIDS Surveillance Report, 2003.

19. Ibid.

Step Three: Be Committed

1. Interview with Dr. Freda McKissic Bush, August 8, 2002.

2. Cynthia Dailard, "Recent Findings from the 'Add Health' Survey: Teens and Sexual Activity," *The Guttmacher Report on Public Policy.* August 2001.

3. "Abstinence – Is It Right for You Now?" on http.//www.teenwire.com.

4. Joyce, "The Ups and Downs of Using Condoms" on http://www.teenwire.com.

5. Paz-Bailey, G., et. al. The effect of correct and consistent condom use on chlamydial and gonococcal infection among urban adolescents. Arch Pediatr Adolesc Med. 2005;159:536-542.

6. Hatcher, R.A., et al. Contraceptive Technology. New York: Ardent Media, INC. 2004.

7. Ibid.

8. Ibid.

9. Ibid. See page 229 for calculation.

10. Centers for Disease Control and Prevention. Male Latex Condoms and Sexually Transmitted Diseases. August 2004. Retrieved November 2005 at http://www.cdc.gov/nchstp/od/latex.htm.

11. National Institutes of Health, Workshop Summary: Scientific Evidence of Condom Effectiveness for STD prevention, 2001.

12. Crosby, R.A. et al. Value of consistent condom use: a study of sexually transmitted disease prevention among African American adolescent females. American Journal of Public Health. June 2003, Vol 93, No. 6.

13. Centers for Disease Control and Prevention. Male Latex Condoms and Sexually Transmitted Diseases. August 2004. Retrieved November 2005 at http://www.cdc.gov/nchstp/od/latex.htm.

14. National Institutes of Health, Workshop Summary: Scientific Evidence of Condom Effectiveness for STD prevention, 2001.

15. Centers for Disease Control and Prevention. Tracking the hidden epidemics, 2000: Trends in the United States. Retrieved November 2005 from http://www.cdc.gov/nchstp/od/news/RevBrochure1pdf.htm.

16. The Alan Guttmacher Institute, Sex and America's Teenagers, New York, AGI, 1994. Calculated by AGI on the basis of data from the Centers for Disease Control and Prevention, Division of HIV/STD prevention, 1992 Annual Report, Atlanta, 1993; Forrest and Singh, 1990; Harlap, Kost, and Forrest, 1991; Sonenstein, Pleck and Ku, 1989; U.S. Bureau of the Census, 1990.

17. J.E. Anderson, R. Wilson, L. Doll, T.S. Jones, P. Barker. "Condom use and HIV risk behaviors among U.S. adults: Data from a nation survey." *Family Planning Perspective.* 1999; 31:24-28.

18. Ibid.

19. Rector, R., Martin, S., and Pardue, M, "Comprehensive Sex Education vs. Authentic Abstinence, A Study of Competing Curricula," The Heritage Foundation, Washington, D.C. 2004.

184

20. Joyce, "Outercourse: Abstinence for Experts" on http://www.teenwire.com.

21. Centers for Disease Control and Prevention. Genital HPV Fact Sheet. Retrieved November 2005 from http://www.cdc.gov/std/healthcomm/fact_sheets.htm.

Discussion Three – Abstinence and "Safe Sex"

1. *Sex, Lies and the Truth*, Focus on the Family. (Video)

2. Hatcher, R.A., et al. Contraceptive Technology. New York: Ardent Media, INC. 2004.

3. Ibid. See page 229 for calculation.

4. National Institutes of Health, Workshop Summary: Scientific Evidence of Condom Effectiveness for STD prevention, 2001.

5. Crosby, R.A. et al. Value of consistent condom use: a study of sexually transmitted disease prevention among African American adolescent females. American Journal of Public Health. June 2003, Vol 93, No. 6.

6. Centers for Disease Control and Prevention. Male Latex Condoms and Sexually Transmitted Diseases. August 2004. Retrieved November 2005 at http://www.cdc.gov/nchstp/od/latex.htm.

7. National Institutes of Health, Workshop Summary: Scientific Evidence of Condom Effectiveness for STD prevention, 2001.

Step Four: Stress the Rewards

1. "Ohno's school of hard knocks," MSNBC News, February 20, 2002.

2. Mark Starr, "Sarah-Dipity!" *Newsweek*, March 4, 2001.

3. "Teen Attitudes about Marriage and Family," *Parent News for January-February 2000*. National Marriage Project, Rutgers University, New Jersey.

4. Glenn Stanton, "Why Marriage Matters," Smart Marriages Archive reproduced in the *Divorce Statistics Collection*.

5. "Teen Attitudes," National Marriage Project.

6. Centers for Disease Control and Prevention and U.S. Department of Health and Human Services: Office of Communication. "New Report Sheds Light on Trends and Patterns in Marriage, Divorce, and Cohabitation," July 23, 2002.

7. David Popenoe and Barbara Dafoe Whitehead, "Should We Live Together: What Young Adults Need to Know about Cohabitation before Marriage" National Marriage Project, Rutgers University, New Jersey. January 1999.

8. Ibid.

9. Helena Oliviero, "Living together: More Americans see what once was called playing house as a step toward or replacement for marriage," *The Atlanta Journal-Constitution*, July 31, 2002.

10. Popenoe and Dafoe, "Should We Live Together?"

11. Janice Crouse, "Is a Marriage License 'Just a Piece of Paper'?" *The Washington Times*, March 18, 2001.

12. Bridget Maher, "Marriage: Key to Happiness," Family Research Council Web Site 2002.

13. "Christianity Today Marriage and Divorce Survey Report," CT Inc. Research Department, July 1992 as reported by the Family Research Council.

14. Mark Clements, *Parade*, August 7, 1994, 4-5, as reported by the Family Research Council.

15. William R. Mattox, Jr., "What's Marriage Got to Do With It?" *Family Policy*, Vol. 6, February 1994 as reported by the Family Research Council.

16. Maher.

17. Stanton.

18. Killam.

19. Peter S. Bearman and Hannah Bruckner, "Promising the Future: Virginity Pledges and First Intercourse," The University of Columbia, 2001.

Discussion Four – Identify the Rewards

1. *Taking Charge*, Human Relations Media. (Video)

2. Ibid.

3. *Real People: Teens Who Choose Abstinence.* (Video)

4. *It's Your Choice*, Human Relations Media. (Video)

5. Ibid.

Step Five: Be There!

1. *Real People: Sex Too Soon*, Sunburst Technology Corp. (Video)

2. Ibid.

3. *Real People: Teen Mothers and Fathers Speak Out*, Sunburst Technology Corp. (Video)

4. "The Green Book," House Committee on Ways and Means, 106th Congress, 2000, Table G-5.

5. Timothy J. Dailey, Ph.D. "Breaking the Ties That Bind: The APA's Assault on Fatherhood." Family Research Council, 1999.

6. Dailey and "The Difference a Dad Makes: Father Facts," *Modern Man*, May 3, 2001.

7. *Modern Man.*

8. Robert. L. Maginnis, "Challenges to Children's Well-Being: Fathers and Parental Time." Speech to the World Congress of Families II, November 14-17, 1999. Family Research Council.

9. National Fatherhood Initiative. "Top Ten Father Facts." in *Father Facts, 4th Edition.* Gaithersburg, Md.: National Fatherhood Initiative, 2002.

10. "Study: Teen girls who are close to mom are less likely to have sex early," *USA Today*, September 4, 2002.

11. Diane Chambers, "Your Ex, Your Child's Other," SingleRose.com. June 28, 2001.

12. Public Broadcasting System in coproduction with 10/20 Productions, LLC. "The Lost Children of Rockdale County," for *Frontline*, 1st broadcast October 19, 1999. (Script and Video)

13. Ibid.

14. Ibid.

15. Ibid.

16. Ibid.

17. Ibid.

18. Ibid.

19. Ibid.

20. Ibid.

21. Ibid.

22. Dailard.

Discussion Five – Being There

1. PBS, "Lost Children."

2. Ibid.

3. Ibid.

Step Six: Build Self-Esteem

1. *Real People: Sex Too Soon.* (Video)

2. Ibid.

3. Ibid.

4. J.M. Spencer, G.D. Zimet, M.C. Aalsma, D.P. Orr. "Self-Esteem as a Predictor of Initiation of Coitus in Early Adolescents." *Pediatrics.* 109:4, April 2002, 581-584.

5. Robert Reasoner, "The True Meaning of Self-Esteem," *National Association for Self-Esteem (NASE).* http://www.self-esteem-nase.org/whatisselfesteem.shtml.

6. B. C. Miller, M.C. Norton, T. Curtis, E.J. Hill, P. Schvaneveldt,, M.H. Young. "The timing of sexual intercourse among adolescents: Family, peers, and other antecedents," *Youth and Society.* 1997: 29:54-83.

7. Anna Quindlen, "Public & Private: The Good Guys," *The New York Times.* April 11, 1993, 4-13.

Discussion Six – Building Self-Esteem

1. *Real People: Sex Too Soon.* (Video)

2. Ibid.

Step Seven: Talk About Relationships

1. Kaiser Family Foundation. "New Study Finds Kids Spend Equivalent of Full Work Week Using Media." November 17, 1999.

2. *Taking Charge.* (Video)

3. *Teen Files.* (Video)

4. Ibid.

5. *Taking Charge.* (Video)

6. Ibid.

7. *Real People: Sex Too Soon.* (Video)

8. Ibid.

9. Elizabeth Thomson and Ugo Coella, "Cohabitation and Marital Stability. Quality or Commitment?" *Journal of Marriage and the Family*, Vol. 54, 1992:256-267.

10. *Real People: Teens Who Choose Abstinence.* (Video)

11. *No Apologies.* (Video)

12. Maher.

Discussion Seven – Relationships

1. *Taking Charge.* (Video)

2. Ibid.

3. *Real People: Teens Who Choose Abstinence.* (Video)

4. Ibid.

Step Eight: Establish Rules and Boundaries

1. Siri Carpenter, "Teens' risky behavior is about more than race and family resources," *Monitor on Psychology*, Vol. 32, No. 1, January 2001.

2. PBS, "Lost Children."

3. Ibid.

4. Ibid.

5. B.P. Yawn and R. A. Yawn, "Adolescent pregnancy: A preventable consequence?" *The Prevention Researcher*, (Winter 1997) Vol. 4 No.1.

6. Kaiser, "Teen Sexual Activity."

7. J.C. Abma, A. Chandra, W.D. Mosher, L. Peterson, L Piccinino. "Fertility, family planning, and women's health: new data from the 1995 National Survey of Family Growth," National Center for Health Statistics: Vital Health Stat 23 (19), 1997.

8. Child Trends Data: National Longitudinal Survey of Youth 1997, (NLSY97), Waves 1-4.

9. PBS, "Lost Children."

10. Walt Mueller, *Understanding Today's Youth Culture*. Wheaton: Tyndale House Publishers, Inc., 1999.

Discussion Eight – Freedom Within Boundaries

1. Child Trends Data: National Longitudinal Survey of Youth 1997, (NLSY97), Waves 1-4.

Step Nine: Teach Refusal Skills

1. *No Apologies.* (Video)

2. Ibid.

3. *Real People: Teens Who Choose Abstinence.* (Video)

4. *It's Your Choice.* (Video)

5. *Taking Charge.* (Video)

6. Kaiser / *seventeen*, "Decision-Making."

7. Ibid.

8. Kaiser / *YM*.

9. Ibid.

10. Kaiser, "Substance Use."

11. Kaiser / *seventeen*, "Decision Making."

12. *Taking Charge.* (Video)

13. Ibid.

14. Ibid.

15. Ibid.

Discussion Nine – Learning How to Say "NO"

1. *No Apologies.* (Video)

2. *Real People: Teens Who Choose Abstinence.* (Video)

3. *It's Your Choice.* (Video)

4. *Taking Charge.* (Video)

Step Ten: Practice Unconditional LOVE

1. *No Apologies.* (Video)

2. Ibid.

3. Ibid.

4. Ibid.

5. Ibid.

6. Ibid.

7. Ibid.

8. Quotes and copy are based on Melody's story as told in *Real People: Teens Who Choose Abstinence.* (Video)

9. Kaiser, "Teen Sexual Activity."

10. *Real People: Sex Too Soon.* (Video)

11. Ibid.

12. Ibid.

13. *Real People: Teen Mothers and Fathers Speak Out.* (Video)

Discussion Ten – Keeping the Communication Lines Open

1. *No Apologies.* (Video)

2. Ibid.

Appendix

Appendix A: *Choosing the Best* Teen Survey

Appendix B: Sexually Transmitted Diseases (photos)

Appendix A

Choosing the Best Teen Survey

1. To what degree did your concern for *contracting an STD* (Sexually Transmitted Disease) influence your decision to be abstinent?

   ❏ -1 Not at all
   ❏ -2 Very little
   ❏ -3 Somewhat
   ❏ -4 Very much
   ❏ -5 A major reason

List the most common STDs (Sexually Transmitted Diseases), their symptoms and whether there is a cure.

_____

_____

_____

2. To what degree did your concern for *becoming pregnant* (or causing a pregnancy) influence your decision to be abstinent?

   ❏ -1 Not at all
   ❏ -2 Very little
   ❏ -3 Somewhat
   ❏ -4 Very much
   ❏ -5 A major reason

What do you think about the "safe-sex" message that states: "Condoms are effective in preventing pregnancy and STDs, if used consistently and correctly"?

_____

_____

_____

3. To what degree did your concern for *emotional consequences* (worry, anxiety, loss of self-respect, etc.) influence your decision to be abstinent?

❏ -1 Not at all
❏ -2 Very little
❏ -3 Somewhat
❏ -4 Very much
❏ -5 A major reason

4. To what degree did your concern for *reaching future goals* in your life influence your decision to be abstinent?

❏ -1 Not at all
❏ -2 Very little
❏ -3 Somewhat
❏ -4 Very much
❏ -5 A major reason

List several goals in your life that remaining abstinent will help you accomplish:

_____

_____

_____

5. To what degree did your concern for *preparing for a future marriage* relationship influence your decision to be abstinent?

❏ -1 Not at all
❏ -2 Very little
❏ -3 Somewhat
❏ -4 Very much
❏ -5 A major reason

6. To what degree did your *religious beliefs* influence your decision to be abstinent?

❏ -1 Not at all
❏ -2 Very little
❏ -3 Somewhat
❏ -4 Very much
❏ -5 A major reason

7. To what degree did *parental expectations* influence your decision to be abstinent?

❏ -1 Not at all
❏ -2 Very little
❏ -3 Somewhat
❏ -4 Very much
❏ -5 A major reason

8. What were your parent(s) expectations concerning sex before marriage?

_____

_____

_____

9. Identify specific ways your parents communicated their expectations to you?

_____

_____

_____

10. List the *top three reasons* you are choosing to be abstinent:

_____

_____

_____

11. How would you describe your relationship with your parents?

_____

_____

_____

12. To what degree do your parent(s) *affirm you* as a person, i.e. make you feel special and cared for?

❏ -1 Not at all
❏ -2 Very little
❏ -3 Somewhat
❏ -4 Very much
❏ -5 Out of sight

Identify specific ways your parent(s) have affirmed you:

_____

_____

_____

13. To what degree do your parent(s) show affection to you?

   ❏ -1 Not at all
   ❏ -2 Very little
   ❏ -3 Somewhat
   ❏ -4 Very much
   ❏ -5 Out of sight

List specific ways your parent(s) shows affection:

_____

_____

_____

14. To what degree have *rules* given to you by your parent(s) helped you in *maintaining your abstinence?*

   ❏ -1 Not at all
   ❏ -2 Very little
   ❏ -3 Somewhat
   ❏ -4 Very much
   ❏ -5 A major help

List some of the rules your parents have established that are helping you maintain your abstinence (dating, curfews, etc.):

_____

_____

_____

15. List any specific achievements or accomplishments that you are proud of:

_____

_____

_____

16. Are you now, or have you been involved in a meaningful, romantic relationship with a member of the opposite sex? If yes:

a) Have you established boundaries for your sexual activity? If so, what are they?

_____

_____

_____

b) Have you ever felt pressured to go farther, or do something sexual, that you didn't want to do? If so, how did you handle it?

_____

_____

_____

c) Do you think there is a difference between love and sex? If so, describe the difference?

_____

_____

_____

17. Have you ever felt pressure from your friends and peers to be sexually active? If so, how did you handle it?

_____

_____

_____

18. Do you have close friends who are committed to help you remain abstinent? If so, to what degree have they helped you remain abstinent?

❑ -1 Not at all
❑ -2 Very little
❑ -3 Somewhat
❑ -4 Very much
❑ -5 A major reason

19. Are you involved in a church or religious youth group? If so, to what degree has your involvement in the group helped you remain abstinent?

❏ -1 Not at all
❏ -2 Very little
❏ -3 Somewhat
❏ -4 Very much
❏ -5 A major reason

20. What are the greatest pressures you face in remaining abstinent until marriage?

_____

_____

_____

21. Have you ever had a sex education course in school that encouraged you to be sexually abstinent?_____

1. If so, how many years and/or sessions did you have? _____

2. What was the name of the material/program?

_____

3. Was it helpful? _____ If so, how?

_____

_____

22. If your younger brother or sister was thinking about having sex and you believed waiting until marriage is the best, write a letter encouraging him or her to stay abstinent until marriage. In your letter, give reasons that you think your brother or sister should wait.

Dear _____,

_____

_____

_____

_____

_____

_____

_____

23. What state do you live in? _____

24. To what degree do you drink alcohol?

- ❏ $^{-1}$ Not at all
- ❏ $^{-2}$ Very little
- ❏ $^{-3}$ Somewhat
- ❏ $^{-4}$ Very much

25. To what degree do you use illegal drugs?

❏   Not at all
❏   Very little
❏   Somewhat
❏   Very much

Thank you for completing the survey!!!

Appendix B

Sexually Transmitted Diseases

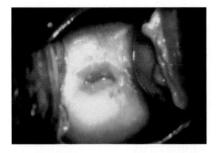

Figure 1

Figure 1 shows a healthy cervix.

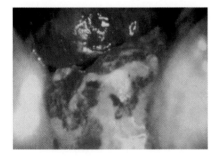

Figure 2

Figure 2 shows a cervix that is infected by **chlamydia**. The infection has caused swelling, redness, and tenderness. Pus drips from the cervix.

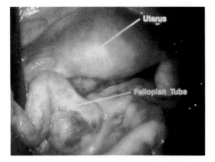

Figure 3

Figure 3 shows the damage of **pelvic inflammatory disease (PID)**. This is a fallopian tube that has been stained blue so you can see how scarring blocks the egg.

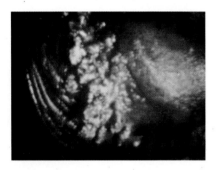

Figure 4

This picture shows a male with genital warts, which can be produced by the **human papillomavirus (HPV)**. Genital warts are small growths on the outside or inside of the genital area.

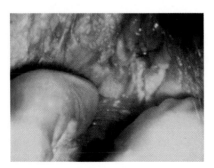

Figure 5

This picture shows a female with genital warts, which can be produced by the **human papillomavirus (HPV)**. Genital warts are small growths on the outside or inside of the genital area.

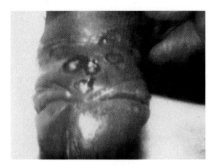

Figure 6

This picture shows a male with **genital herpes.** A blister on the skin's surface is a sign that the virus is active.

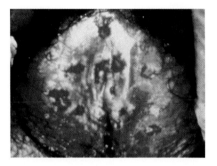

Figure 7

This picture shows a female with **genital herpes.** A blister on the skin's surface is a sign that the virus is active.

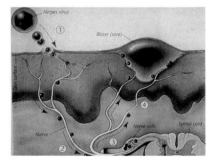

Figure 8

This picture shows how **genital herpes** attacks the body. After the blister opens and "weeps," it will dry up. Then, the virus moves along the nerve cells and lodges near the spine. Any kind of stress can bring the virus back to the surface where it again forms blisters.